RELIGIOUS WOMEN IN MED[

© Roberta Gilchrist and Marilyn Oliva 1993

ISBN 0 906219 36 1

All rights reserved. No part of this publication may be reproduced, stored in a retrieval system, or transmitted, in any form or by any means, electronic, mechanical, or otherwise, without permission of the Authors.

Published by the Centre of East Anglian Studies, University of East Anglia, Norwich, NR4 7TJ.
Printed by the Printing Unit, University of East Anglia.
Cover design by UEA Design Studio.

Front cover: Prioress's seal from Bungay, Suffolk, c1300. Reproduced with permission of the British Library (seal LXXI.89 9250237).

Table of Contents

List of Figures, Plates and Tables	6
Abbreviations	7
Acknowledgements	8
Introduction	9
Chapter 1: The Tradition of Female Piety in East Anglia	13
Chapter 2: Monasteries for Women in Norfolk and Suffolk	23
Chapter 3: The Nuns of Norfolk and Suffolk	46
Chapter 4: Piety and Patronage	57
Chapter 5: Informal Communities and Individual Ascetics	68
Chapter 6: Conclusion	81
Archaeological Gazetteer of East Anglian Nunneries	83
Tables	93
Bibliography	102
Index	112

List of Figures

Figure 1: Distribution of Female Religious in Medieval Norfolk
Figure 2: Distribution of Female Religious in Medieval Suffolk
Figure 3: Reconstruction of Crabhouse Priory in 1557
Figure 4: Illustration of a Corbel at Marham Abbey
Figure 5: Plan of Carrow Priory

List of Plates

Plate 1: Prioress's Seal from Bungay Priory (c1300)
Plate 2: Aerial View of Marham Abbey
Plate 3: North Gable at Redlingfield Priory
Plate 4: Redlingfield Parish Church and Monastic Building
Plate 5: Aerial View of Carrow Priory, c1932-9
Plate 6: Bungay Priory, Remains with Parish Church
Plate 7: Marham Abbey, Aerial View of Church
Plate 8: Thetford Priory, Remains of Church and Chapter-house
Plate 9: Aerial photograph showing cropmarks at Abbey Farm, Shouldham
Plate 10: West Range at Campsey Ash Priory
Plate 11: Elmhill, Norwich

List of Tables

Table 1: Monasteries for Women in the Diocese of Norwich
Table 2: Hospitals Staffed by Women in the Diocese of Norwich
Table 3: Informal Communities of Religious Women in the Diocese of Norwich
Table 4: Anchoress's Sites in the Diocese of Norwich
Table 5: Vowesses in the Diocese of Norwich
Table 6: Other Religious Women in the Diocese of Norwich

Abbreviations

Sources:

Add Ms	Additional Manuscript
ANF	Archdeaconry of Norfolk
ANW	Archdeaconry of Norwich
ASF	Archdeaconry of Suffolk
BL	Bradfer-Lawrence
DN/REG	Diocese of Norwich Bishops' Register
DCN	Dean and Chapter of Norwich
NCC	Norwich Consistory Court
NCP	Norwich Cathedral Priory
PCC	Perogative Court of Canterbury
Stowe Ch	Stowe Charter

Record Repositories:

BL	British Library
NRO	Norfolk Record Office
PRO	Public Record Office
SRO	Suffolk Record Office

Publications:

CCR	Calendar of Close Rolls
CPL	Calendar of Papal Letters
CPR	Calendar of Patent Rolls
EHR	English Historical Review
NA	Norfolk Archaeology
PSIA	Proceedings of the Suffolk Institute of Archaeology
TV	Testamenta Vetusta
VCH	Victoria County History
VE	Valor Ecclesiasticus

Acknowledgements

The authors would like to thank the following people and institutions for their support and contributions to this publication: Hassell Smith, Mavis Wesley, Roger Virgoe, Carole Rawcliffe and Richard Wilson at the Centre of East Anglian Studies; Norman Scarfe and the Norman Scarfe Charitable Trust; Rachel Farmer, Frank Meeres, and Paul Rutledge at the Norfolk Record Office; the Norfolk and Suffolk Sites and Monuments Records; Derek A. Edwards of Norfolk Museums Service Landscape Archaeology Section for aerial photographs; Christopher Harper-Bill, Mary Erler, Elizabeth Garity, Ruth Harvey, T.A. Heslop, Peter Northeast and Judith Middleton-Stewart. Drawings are by Philip Judge and Ted West (Figure 4). The seal of Bungay Priory is reproduced by permission of the British Library.

Introduction

Women played a prominent role in the spiritual life of medieval England. Anchoresses, mystics, and nuns are perhaps the most familiar among women whose vocations encompassed lives of prayer and service to others (Warren 1985; Power 1922). But other forms of religious life were also pursued by women in the Middle Ages. Many of these options were part of a long-established tradition of female Christian piety which continued to flourish throughout the Middle Ages, whether condemned or condoned by the Church hierarchy.

The medieval diocese of Norwich, which comprised the counties of Norfolk and Suffolk, supported what appears to have been a disproportionately large population of religious women. Some, for example nuns and anchoresses, lived their vocations within the institutional framework of the Church. Other women created their own religious lifestyles to nurture the spiritual needs which were otherwise overlooked by the traditional Church hierarchy. The preponderance of female religious in medieval Norfolk and Suffolk adds a significant dimension to what historians have previously noted about the diocese: that in the Middle Ages the lay population of Norfolk and Suffolk were active participants in, and generous supporters of, a dynamic religious culture. Indeed, this particular aspect of East Anglian society has come to characterise the region (Aston 1984; Tanner 1984).

This book examines the options available to women who chose a religious life in the diocese of Norwich between the eleventh and the sixteenth centuries. Chapter 1 offers a brief survey of the variety of both communal and individual religious lifestyles which women followed, and addresses some of the historiographical problems which have traditionally beset studies of medieval religious women. Chapters 2 through 5 provide more detailed discussions of the religious lifestyles of women in East Anglia, including the material culture and secular society which supported them. By placing the nuns, hospital sisters, anchoresses, vowesses, and others in the broader

Introduction

context of the lay communities of which they were integral parts, this examination reveals the tight web of interactions which both sustained the religious women and spiritually nurtured lay society throughout the period.

Tables at the end of this book provide basic information about the types of religious women: their locations, the dates they occurred, and the sources from which our information has been drawn. Full citations to both primary and secondary sources for these tables can be found in the list of abbreviations and the bibliography.

Abundant documentary and archaeological evidence exists which sheds light on these women and indicates how they were perceived by contemporary lay society. The best documented religious women in the diocese are the nuns, who thus comprise a significant portion of this study. Monastic household accounts inventory food and supplies bought and sold; bishops' visitation records provide a window through which to view the veracity of religious vocations among the diocese's nuns. Documents like these enable us to determine the quality of life within the convents, while archaeological sources, sixteenth-century inventories, and the nuns' books and monastic seals allow us to recreate the physical realities of daily life and the more symbolic meanings of the architecture and landscapes of monasteries for women.

Perhaps wills are the most revealing sources for women in medieval East Anglia who pursued a religious life outside the confines of a cloister: anchoresses, vowesses, and members of informal communities of religious women. While only a few wills date from the thirteenth century, significantly more survive from the 1300s, and thousands are extant for the fifteenth and sixteenth centuries. The most useful wills were probated in several diocesan courts: the Consistory Court, and the four archdeaconry courts, Norfolk, Norwich, Sudbury, and Suffolk. In general, wills probated in these courts represent different levels of medieval society. Those people who held land in more than one archdeaconry had their wills probated in the Consistory Court; those with more local landholdings went to the appropriate archdeaconry court. In addition to providing the evidence for the existence of many of the female religious surveyed here, bequests from testators from different social ranks indicate how people viewed religious women, and provide us with an insight into how these religious women affected various levels of society within the diocese.

While some of the information presented here has been known to

Introduction

previous monastic and local historians, we have uncovered and harnessed new material which enlightens our understanding of medieval religious women. By examining all of the religious lifestyles for women in a single study we have revealed a landscape of female piety in medieval East Anglia hitherto unrecognised. Our research has also alerted us to characteristics of female piety which were specifically gender-related. That is, we can now identify certain aspects of the religious life of medieval women in East Anglia which were not shared by their male counterparts, but which can be found among religious women in other parts of medieval England, in the early Church, and in other religious traditions.

Finally, when appropriate, we compare the religious women of medieval Norfolk and Suffolk with their male counterparts, and place these holy women in the wider context of female piety in medieval England. We hope that the findings presented here will stimulate similar regional studies of nuns, hospital sisters, anchoresses and other religious women.

Chapter 1
The Tradition of Female Piety in East Anglia

Female piety was an active force in the religious world of the Middle Ages. As recent work has shown, this piety emphasised a denial and denigration of the physical body and a particular attraction to Christ and his suffering on the Cross (Bynum 1982; Bynum 1987). These characteristics of female piety were reflected in a number of lifestyles which religious women chose, and were poignantly expressed in the writings and revelations of various female saints and mystics. Perhaps the best known female mystics are Margery Kemp and Julian of Norwich; both lived in medieval East Anglia.

These two women enjoyed a high public profile during their lifetimes and have attracted the attentions of later historians. Hundreds of other women less visible to subsequent historians also pursued religious lifestyles in medieval Norfolk and Suffolk. These lifestyles included women who lived in communities and those who desired more solitary lives. Some of these options required vows and a formal affiliation with the institutional Church, such as cloistered nuns, hospital sisters and anchoresses. Vowesses and other women chose a less formal association with a monastery for women or parish church.

At least six categories of religious women existed in medieval East Anglia. The first three categories correspond with women who lived communally, and includes nuns who lived in monasteries for women, hospital sisters, and groups of women who established informal religious communities. Women who observed more solitary vocations included anchoresses, vowesses, and other religious women who are more difficult to define retrospectively. Maps of Norfolk and Suffolk show the locations of each of the six categories of religious women in the diocese (Figures 1 and 2).

The best documented and most easily recognisable female religious were the choir, or cloistered, nuns who lived in monastic communities and followed a specific monastic rule or order. Of the eleven monasteries for women (or nunneries) in the diocese of Norwich, five were Benedictine houses, the most popular monastic order in England, and three convents followed the rule of St Augustine (Table 1) (Knowles 1941, 1, 9-10). The remaining three female monasteries were affiliated with different orders: Marham was a Cistercian house; Bruisyard a convent of Poor Clares; and Shouldham was a Gilbertine priory for both nuns and canons. This distribution according to order was representative of the female houses in the rest of medieval England: roughly half of the 136 convents were Benedictine priories; eighteen per cent of the English female monasteries were Cistercian foundations; fifteen per cent followed the Augustinian Rule; and eleven per cent were Gilbertine double houses (Power 1922, 1). The rest of the English convents were associated with the Cluniac, Premonstratension, Bridgettine and Dominican orders, and with the orders of Fontrevault and the Poor Clares (Franciscans).

Subtle distinctions marked each of these monastic orders, but they all demanded a communal lifestyle. Members of these communities shared a common dormitory and meals, and participated in several hours of communal prayer. Women who desired to live this type of religious life also took vows of poverty, obedience, and chastity: vows which both permanently removed them from secular society, and also signalled a special status as women devoted to a life of prayer. Spiritually removed from secular society, the nuns were also physically separated from lay people by their monasteries' precincts, from which they could venture on few occasions.

Another option for a woman who desired to lead a religious life in community with others was to become a hospital sister (Table 2). These women also took religious vows, and while their vocations also called for daily prayer, their primary focus was tending the sick and poor. We know a great deal less about these sisters than we do about their cloistered counterparts. We do know, however, that one could either be a 'whole sister' or a 'half sister', terms which medieval will-makers used to describe them. In 1385, for example, Bartholomew of Appleyard, citizen of Norwich, left 12*d.* to the '*sorores intregalis*' and the '*sorores dimidies*' (NRO, NCC 68 Harsyk). This distinction indicates a degree of regulation in the religious life which hospital sisters might pursue. Perhaps the 'whole sisters' lived

Female Piety

Figure 1: Distribution of Female Religious in Medieval Norfolk (see Tables 1-6).

Female Piety

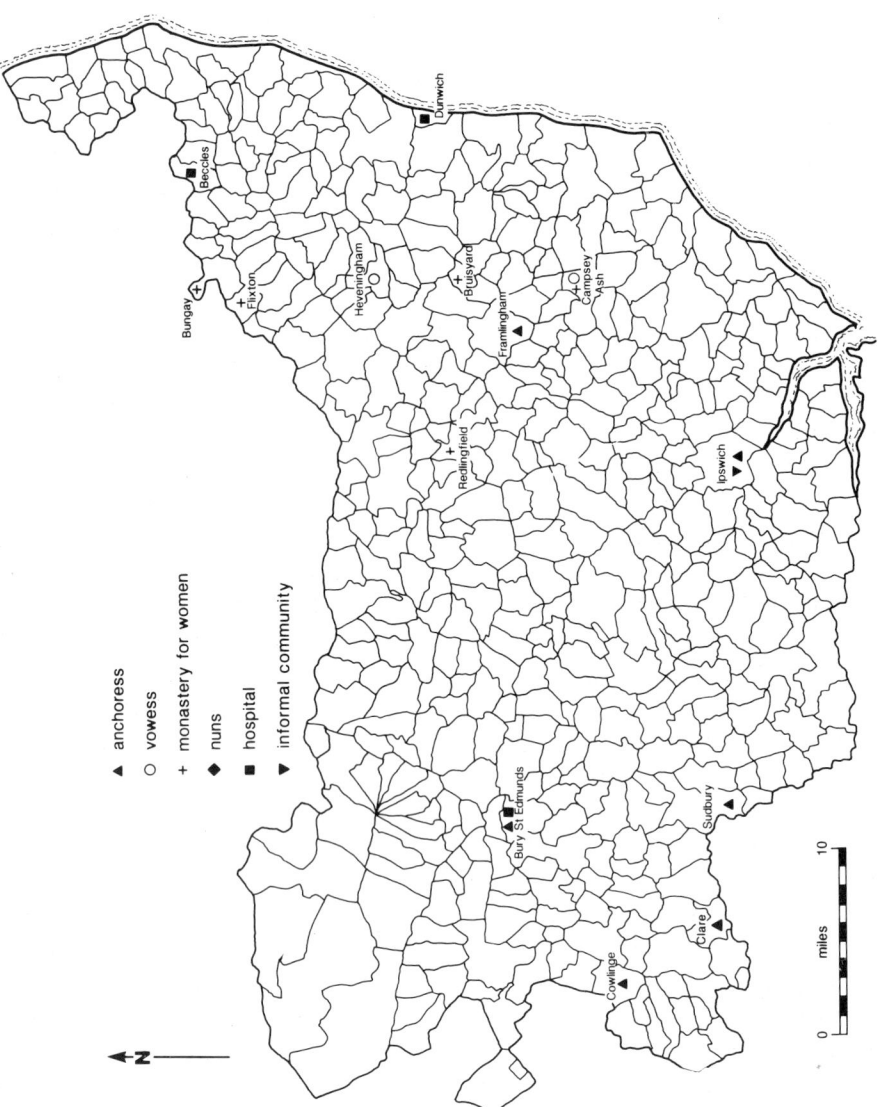

Figure 2: Distribution of Female Religious in Medieval Suffolk (see Tables 1-6).

within the hospital buildings, while the 'half sisters' returned to their homes after caring for hospital inmates.

While both cloistered nuns and hospital sisters comprised part of the institutional medieval Church, other groups of women in East Anglia lived together in less formal religious communities (Table 3). Fifteenth- and sixteenth-century wills provide evidence that in at least four parishes in the city of Norwich, and in the town of Ipswich, groups of women lived together under a self-imposed vow of chastity or poverty. Between 1427 and 1445, for example, *'sorores castitati dedicate'* lived in the parish of St Swithin's in Norwich in a tenement of John Pellet (Tanner 1984, 203; Taylor 1821, 65). These communities did not follow a monastic rule and do not appear to have been recognised by Church authorities. What is interesting about these informal communities is that they appear to have been unique to East Anglia; no other examples of this type of female religious community have been found in other parts of medieval England.

Living in a community offered women a special status and a sense of solidarity with other like-minded individuals. Such communities also allowed women to develop and be rewarded for administrative skills by offering them higher positions on a career ladder of administrative offices (Chapter 3). The evidence for this meritocracy is strongest for the nuns (about whom we know the most) (Oliva 1990), but it is likely that the opportunities to hold similar offices and advance to higher ones was present in medieval hospitals and perhaps in the informal parochial communities in Norwich and Ipswich.

While all medieval women were responsible for administering their households, and certain categories of lay women also managed careers, alewives and participants in certain textile trades in particular, secular women were forever bound by legal and economic restraints imposed by medieval society. Even though nuns and hospital sisters lived under the dominance of the institutional Church, they enjoyed a certain measure of independence unknown to their secular counterparts. These religious women not only managed their busy households and complicated finances without male supervision or interference, they also decided upon and executed the activities which wed them to their local lay communities. The diocese's female monastic superiors, for instance, accepted corrodians (lifetime paying guests) and other lay people to live as permanent residents within their monastic precincts, and boarded temporary guests, including children, who were usually also taught by the nuns. In addition, superiors and rank and file nuns acted as witnesses and executrices of the wills of local people (Oliva 1994, forthcoming).

Despite the advantages of a communal religious lifestyle, many women sought a more solitary means to fulfill their pious vocations. The most severely ascetic of the individual religious lifestyles available to medieval women was that of an anchoress, like Julian of Norwich. Recent findings indicate that the majority of anchorites in medieval England were female (Warren 1985, 19-21); and it appears that a disproportionately large number of these solitary women lived in East Anglia (Table 4). Like the religious women in communities, anchoresses also took vows, but these holy women were further removed from society by being walled in - literally buried alive - in small cells attached to a church, with only a small grill, or narrow slit, through which they received food and communicated with the outside world. Medieval society placed a high value on these solitary ascetics for the severity of their lifestyles and for the prayers they sang for the benefit of all.

Similar in lifestyle to an anchoress was a female hermit (included in Table 4). These women too desired solitary lives, but rather than take official church vows, female hermits (there is no female form of this word) struck out on their own and followed the model of the Desert Church Fathers and Harlots. Like an anchoress, a vital part of a hermit's vocation was to live away from society in an uninhabitable place where one could lead an isolated life of prayer. Though there were no deserts in medieval England, the fens and marshlands of western Norfolk, as well as the suburbs of towns like Norwich, served the same psychological purpose as a desert landscape by being remote or removed, wild, and inhospitable places for human life. Perhaps it is not surprising to find the majority of the diocese's female hermits and anchoresses in the western fens of Norfolk and around the city of Norwich.

Less austere and less far removed from society, the vowess was another popular religious lifestyle available to medieval women (Table 5). These women were widows who, in the presence of a bishop, were veiled and given a ring to denote their special status. They also vowed to lead chaste and prayerful lives, either within a female monastic house, or, more commonly, remaining in their own homes. Vowesses were encouraged by the Church hierarchy because their non-married status aligned them with virgins, the most highly valued women in the eyes of the Christian Church (McLaughlin 1974, 222). Vowesses, like the informal communities of religious women, seem to have been a phenomenon of the later medieval period, although the early Church Fathers, Augustine and Jerome, counselled and wrote for such women, indicating a long tradition of this type of religious life (Ruether 1974, 169-173). While we know relatively little about vowesses, their existence has been acknowledged by antiquaries who discovered certain treatises about this religious lifestyle, and descriptions of the ritual whereby a woman was veiled, ringed, and vowed to lead a chaste life of prayer (Harrod 1844; Fosbrooke 1817). The last category of religious women in East Anglia, however, includes individuals and groups that historians have not previously noted (Table 6). Like the informal religious communities, the evidence we have about these women comes from wills.

Among bequests made by sixteenth-century testators to priests, vicars, friars, nuns, almshouses and monasteries, are gifts given to women called 'mother': for example, 'blind Mother Love' in Norwich (NRO, NCC 57-59 Grundisburgh). In addition to these women, several wills, dating from the thirteenth to the sixteenth centuries, mention nuns in places which were neither known female monastic houses nor places which can be identified as nunneries by any other evidence. We discuss in a later chapter the nature of these women's vocations. It is important here to note their existence and acknowledge that by virtue of their placement in the wills among bequests to other religious people and communities, these women also held some type of religious status.

Identifying these rather enigmatic women, and determining their religious significance to their contemporaries, addresses two interrelated issues that bear on any study of medieval religious women: terminology and the historiography of the female religious in general. As a rule, we have maintained the integrity of our sources by calling all of the female religious we have found by the terms used in the documents. Thus, although we do not know the precise religious status of women called 'mother', we use the terms contemporaries used to describe them rather than make assumptions about their status and purpose by automatically assigning them labels, such as god-mothers or ex-nuns. We have done so in order to avoid the confusion which can result when historians affix standard labels of religious life to these and other women. The informal groups of women in Norwich and Ipswich, for example, are referred to by Dunn and Tanner as beguinages (Dunn 1973, 24; Tanner 1984, 66-68, 130-131). A thirteenth-century phenomenon of the Low Countries, beguinages were communities of women who worked, begged, and prayed, outside the formal structure of the Church. We do not know, however, who the women in the Norwich parishes were or what they were doing; we cannot with any certainty say that their lifestyles resembled that of the beguines. The danger in labelling them as such is that it might blind us to their real vocations and true functions, something that admittedly we may never know.

The problem of terminology and definition of vocation impinges upon the study of medieval religious women in general. The standard terminology available to historians to describe the religious lifestyles in the Middle Ages is one created by, and for, the male religious. Monk, friar, canon, anchorite, and hermit, for example, describe a variety of vocations for Christians, and although these lifestyles were pursued by both sexes, the terminology used to describe them is strictly male-oriented. The lack of a female form of the term hermit is a telling index of this male bias. While it is true that the term 'nun' applies to women only, most monastic orders were organised by men for men with little or no consideration of a role for religious women (Kearney 1987).

The absence of a terminology appropriate to female religious has rendered some religious women invisible to later historians. Hitherto, the nuns listed in Table 6 have gone unnoticed, women who apparently lived some sort of communal lives in places which had no formal monastic houses. Likewise, the 'mothers' have never before been included in any discussions of religious life in the diocese. Why have these religious women been omitted from other studies of the spiritual culture of medieval East Anglia?

The answer seems to be that these women do not fit the standard terminology used to describe religious personnel in the Middle Ages. This problem is compounded, moreover, by the implications of the extant terminology used both by the medieval Church and later historians. The male standard which describes religious vocations and lifestyles ascribes a higher value to the male religious than it does to their female counterparts, a sytem of values repeated and fostered by many historians (Southern 1970, 310). It is possible, therefore, that the 'mothers' and nuns were overlooked in other studies of religious life in medieval East Anglia because they did not fit the standard male mould of what constituted acceptable religious lifestyles within the institutional Church.

The persistent use of a male religious standard by historians has not only obscured some of the religious women from our view, it has also contributed to a marginalisation of female religious lifestyles. Many religious women, including, for example, Margery Kemp, have been described by historians as part of a religious fringe because their behaviour did not conform to the ordained Church doctrine (Knowles 1955, viii). And while this application of a male standard does not ignore the formal female monastic houses or hospitals, it does diminish their importance by under-valuing them in relation to their male counterparts (Knowles 1955, 1959; Power 1922, *passim*).

The male religious standard has also prevented us from appreciating certain characteristics of female piety. Without question, it would be far more simple to classify these religious women into ready categories. But the informality and ambiguity of some of the religious women in the diocese of Norwich prohibit us from doing so, for example the women devoted to chastity in Norwich. Indeed, such fluidity was an integral part of female piety and reflected, moreover, the attitudes that the institutional Church held towards women.

The attitude of the Church toward women was at best ambiguous, at worst misogynist. The teachings of the Church Fathers, including Ambrose, Augustine, and Aquinas, combine vitriolic portrayals of women as the descendants of Eve, whose actions condemned humanity to its post-lapsarian condition, with genuine concern and admiration for virgins, women who lived chaste marital lives, and certain female ascetics who stood as exemplary models for all Christians (McNamara 1982; Ruether 1974). We suggest here that such conflicting messages about the status of women affected their spiritual lifestyles, and were reflected in the religious opportunities open to and created by them.

Incorporating the institutionally recognised religious women with the more provisional groups which flourished in medieval Norfolk and Suffolk allows us to see the broad landscape of female piety and its gender-specific characteristics. Such a synthesis of religious women also facilitates an appreciation of the long-standing tradition of female piety throughout the Middle Ages, which seems to have proliferated especially in East Anglia. And while this study focuses primarily on post-Conquest religious women, during the early medieval period a number of female saints emerged who were associated with religious communities in the greater region of East Anglia. St Withburga (d. 743) is believed to have founded a house at West Dereham; St Etheldreda (d. 660) founded the monastery at Ely; St Osyth (d. 653) is associated with Chich in north-east Essex; and the ninth-century saints Pandon and Winfrith are associated with Eltisley in Cambridgeshire. More ascetic connections exist for Peakirk, Cambridgeshire, where according to Felix's *Life of Guthlac*, Pega, the sister of Guthlac, established her own hermitage in the eighth century.

Many more communities of women, or mixed religious houses of women and men, may have existed and yet have remained undocumented. Hints of these sites are occasionally provided through archaeological excavation in which middle Saxon ecclesiastical artefacts are found in association with timber churches and skeletal populations biased toward adults (Gilchrist 1993). The case for Brandon in Suffolk is particularly strong (Carr 1988); additional candidates may be provided in time by archaeological evidence. In the tenth and eleventh centuries, religious women lived together in informal communities or were attached to monasteries for men. Domesday Book for Norfolk lists under the Lands of Isaac 'in Seething a certain poor nun claims 4 acres of land she held under (Earl) Ralph' (II.47.7), and the Suffolk entry for Bury St Edmunds includes '28 nuns and poor persons, who prayed daily for the King and all Christian people' (I.14.167).

The case for a long and flourishing tradition of female piety in medieval East Anglia is persuasive. This study of the diocese's religious women reveals various facets of female piety which contribute both to our knowledge of religious women and also to the history of medieval spirituality. This overview of the tradition of female piety provides the context for more detailed descriptions of the communal and individual lifestyles of women in Norfolk and Suffolk throughout the Middle Ages.

Chapter 2
Monasteries for Women in Norfolk and Suffolk

The diocese of Norwich counted among its religious institutions eleven formal nunneries: Bruisyard Abbey, Bungay, Campsey Ash, Flixton, and Redlingfield Priories in Suffolk, and Blackborough, Carrow, Crabhouse, Shouldham, Thetford Priories, and Marham Abbey in Norfolk. These houses were small, relatively poor foundations which nevertheless maintained consistent numbers of nuns throughout the Middle Ages, and enjoyed a greater percentage of patronage from lay society than their male counterparts (Oliva 1991). To gain an accurate view of the monasteries for women of East Anglia, and of the relationships that they maintained with lay society, we look first at their material culture: dates of foundation, geographic locations, founders, initial endowments, dedications to saints, and the nuns' seigneurial rights and privileges. An analysis of the nunneries' seals and a discussion of their ground-plans and buildings are included in this chapter.

The majority of the monasteries for women in Norfolk and Suffolk were founded in the mid- to late twelfth century, a time of great expansion of female monasticism in England. Between 1130 and 1165, in fact, most of England's female houses were established (Elkins 1988, 45, 118). Like the majority of convents founded at this time, most of those in the diocese of Norwich were rural foundations, geographically clustered in two regions. In the prosperous farming area of High Suffolk were Campsey Ash, Flixton, Redlingfield, and Bruisyard. Blackborough, Crabhouse, Marham, and Shouldham were sited in the western Norfolk fens and Brecklands, areas of light and sandy soil subject to frequent flooding.

Three houses were associated with towns. Carrow was established outside the south walls of the town of Norwich, and Thetford was sited south of the walls of Thetford. This suburban setting was typical of the spatial relationship shared by other English towns and female religious houses, like the convents located outside the city walls of Stamford, Cambridge, Derby, and York (Gilchrist 1993). Thetford Priory was further isolated from the town by its placement within a loop of the River Thet, a setting similar to that of St Radegund's, Cambridge, and St Clement's, York. Bungay Priory's location was less typical of English monasteries for women. Here the convent was founded at the principal parish church of a market town which grew up at the site of a Norman castle.

Most of the Norwich diocesan houses, like their counterparts elsewhere, were founded by lay people of middling social rank (Elkins 1988, 95-7). Five of the nunneries in Norfolk and Suffolk were established by local women: Emma, the daughter and heir of the lord of Redlingfield, founded Redlingfield Priory with part of her inheritance. Similarly, Margery de Creyk used her local holdings to found Flixton Priory; Muriel de Scales established Blackborough. Agnes and Joan de Valoine instituted Campsey Ash, and Leva of Lynn created Crabhouse. The founders of several other monasteries for women in the diocese were people of higher social status. Gundreda de Glanville bestowed properties to institute Bungay. Isabel of Arundel founded Marham Abbey; the Duke of Clarence established Bruisyard Abbey, the last female monastic foundation in the diocese; King Stephen founded Carrow. Geoffrey Fitzpiers initially endowed Shouldham.

Despite the higher social standing of the founders of Marham, Bruisyard, Bungay, and Carrow, the relatively poor economic status of these convents was similar to that of the houses founded by women of lesser social rank (Table 1). Only Campsey Ash and Shouldham ever attained a valuation above £100, suggesting a slight correlation between the social status of a monastery's founder and its later economic development. The relative poverty of the female houses in Norfolk and Suffolk can be explained partly by their small initial endowments, some of which comprised rural areas of marginal land. The initial endowments of Blackborough, Bungay, Crabhouse, and Marham, for example, consisted of small manors, local parish churches, and plots of rather unproductive land. Emma of Redlingfield gave her foundation the manor of Redlingfield and the local parish church. Flixton was founded with comparable properties: Flixton manor and the advowson of the parish church. Neither manor was very large, and none of the attendant endowments were accompanied by land outside their respective parish boundaries.

While meagre initial endowments of mediocre quality clearly limited the convents' economic resources, their poverty and geographic locations provide an insight into the ascetic nature of female piety. In their rural and suburban settings, these female monasteries were located at the margins of society. Indeed, in certain cases the nuns actively sought marginality and isolation, like the earlier ascetics, Guthlac and Pega, who had emulated the Desert Fathers. In medieval East Anglia, the penitential solitude of the desert was found in the fens and marshlands. The Crabhouse Priory cartulary tells us that Leva, a hermit, and her followers sought a desert and solitary place (*heremus*), which they found in the fens of West Norfolk. When Crabhouse was founded, the parish was empty of other inhabitants, and the area was not reclaimed for marshland until the thirteenth century digging of the Old Podike drain (Dymond 1990, 122). Similarly, Isabel of Arundel sought the most isolated and contemplative setting available for her Cistercian foundation at Marham. Thetford, originally a cell of Bury St Edmunds, was considered remote and poor by the few monks who lived there, but was deemed a suitable site for a group of religious women living in Lyng. Finally, the nuns of Bruisyard Abbey actively sought a life of poverty, which was the cornerstone of the order of Poor Clare.

Poverty and isolation, therefore, were not necessarily considered negative attributes by the patrons of female monasticism. Women's religious houses were founded on marginal land or outside town walls not simply as a reflection of their founders' finances, or, as previous historians have suggested, because nuns were valued less by society than monks and canons (Baskerville 1937; Gasquet 1905). Rather, female monastic sites reflected the nature of the piety expressed within and by the houses. Located at the physical and psychological fringes of medieval society, these monasteries for women represented poverty and physical separation from society, both vital aspects of female piety. The convents were also part of an eremetical tradition of female religious which, as later chapters show, flowered in East Anglia in a variety of ways.

If nuns in East Anglia actively sought rural and suburban settings and poverty as aspects of their religious lifestyles, it is not surprising that monasteries for women show little evidence of having altered the landscapes with which they were endowed. While the larger male houses and double monasteries implemented an active reordering of landscapes, particularly in relation to water management and land reclamation, the female houses were either unable to instigate such programmes, or such activities were considered irrelevant to the purpose for which a nunnery was founded. A certain degree of fenland reclamation was carried out by Crabhouse and Blackborough, but the majority of draining seems to have been implemented by neighbouring landlords (Bateson 1892, 9).

In addition to choosing the geographical site and donating properties to their monastic foundations, founders also dedicated religious houses to certain saints. Female monasteries were generally dedicated to the Virgin Mary, sometimes in association with one or more additional saints. East Anglian examples of this first pattern included Campsey Ash and Carrow, which were dedicated solely to the Blessed Virgin Mary, and Bruisyard, which was devoted to the Annunciation. Bruisyard's was a more unusual dedication in keeping with its late foundation date, and referred to the New Testament passage from Luke which describes the angel Gabriel's announcement to the Virgin that she would conceive and bear a son (Luke 1:26-38).

The majority of the East Anglian female houses followed the second pattern of monastic dedications and were jointly consecrated to the Virgin and other saints. Joint dedications included Blackborough and Flixton, devoted to both St Mary the Virgin and St Catherine; Crabhouse, to the Blessed Virgin Mary and St John the Evangelist; and Marham, to St Mary and Sts Barbara and Edmund. Both Shouldham and Bungay Priories were dedicated to the Blessed Virgin Mary and the Holy Cross; Redlingfield, to the Blessed Virgin Mary and St Andrew. Only Thetford formed an exception to these patterns. Its dedication to St George was unusual among monastic devotions, and was generally specific to male monasteries of the Benedictine order (Binns 1989, 34). Thetford's choice of St George as patron referred to the earlier cell of monks belonging to Bury St Edmunds which preceded the female foundation on the same site, and possibly to a parish church recorded at Thetford in Domesday.

Monastic dedications followed certain conventions. The Virgin Mary was by far the most popular patron saint of female and male monasteries of every order. Dedications to St John the Evangelist gained popularity in the twelfth century (*ibid*, 29), contemporary with the foundation of Crabhouse. From the eleventh century devotions to St Andrew, such as Redlingfield, were relatively numerous as well. Dedications to St Catherine were far more unusual, however, and seem to have been confined to double houses, like the Gilbertine foundation in Lincoln, or monasteries for women, like Blackborough, Flixton, and Polsloe, a Benedictine priory near Exeter. Additional chapels were dedicated to St Catherine at Carrow and Blackborough. Marham's joint dedication to Sts Barbara and Edmund is intriguing for a Cistercian foundation, as the order adopted the Virgin as its patron saint. Monastic devotions to St Barbara were rare, although an Augustinian monastery for men at Beckford (Gloucester) was consecrated to her (*ibid*, 102). The dedications to Sts Catherine and Barbara at Blackborough, Flixton, and Marham may reflect a preference for female saints among the women who founded these East Anglian religious houses.

Dedications to the Holy Cross were relatively infrequent also, occurring among male houses of the Augustinian order (Binns 1989, 120). However, the Holy Cross shared joint dedication with the Virgin at Bungay, a Benedictine house, and at the Gilbertine double monastery of Shouldham. While the churches of the nuns and canons at Gilbertine houses were commonly given separate dedications (*ibid*, 29), there is no evidence that this custom was followed at Shouldham.

Founders of monastic institutions established certain basic elements of the religious houses for women in the diocese of Norwich. Included among these factors were substantial seigneurial rights and privileges which often accompanied original grants of land, or were given to the houses by later patrons. These rights increased the nuns' revenues and contributed to their local prestige. As manorial lords, for example, all of the prioresses and abbesses held manor courts which dealt with a variety of business: offences against manorial custom, election of manorial officials, conveyances of land, and personal disputes between the head of the manor and her bond tenants. Carrow and Marham enjoyed the additional right to hold leet courts for both their bond and free tenants, and both houses had the rights to view frankpledge and the assize of bread and ale.

Three of the female houses held special privileges. The prioress of Carrow was exempt from municipal jurisdiction as she held exclusive rights over her lands inside and outside the Norwich town walls. Her peculiar jurisdiction allowed her, among other things, to probate wills and maintain gallows. The abbess of Marham also probated wills and kept gallows; and she could lawfully bury local parishioners in the conventual cemetery. Both Marham and Blackborough, moreover, were legal sanctuaries for accused wrongdoers.

In addition to these seigneurial rights, the female houses enjoyed certain economic privileges associated with their lordly status. Carrow, for example, had the right to hold a four day fair on the vigil, day, and two days following the Nativity of the Blessed Virgin. Shouldham held a weekly market and an annual fair on the feast of St Nicholas at Stoke Ferry, and Blackborough had a fair. Several convents, including Campsey Ash, Crabhouse, and Flixton, had water mills, and Marham had both a water and a fulling mill. In addition to contributing to the convents' incomes, these secular rights and privileges also integrated the female houses into the lives of local people. While it is doubtful that any of the abbesses or prioresses ever personally appeared at their courts, gallows, sanctuaries, or markets and fairs, nevertheless the fines, offences, and tolls were levied, pardoned, and punished in the name of the monastic superiors, thus embedding them in their local lay communities in several important ways.

Like other male monastic and lay landholders, the nuns' manorial status entailed various legal and financial transactions and agreements which were closed and authenticated by the convents' seals. The iconography depicted on the seals reflected both the dedications of the conventual churches and the image of authority chosen to represent the monastery. These seals, and the spiritual symbolism which they reveal, provide perhaps the best surviving evidence for the iconography of nunneries in Norfolk and Suffolk.

As the majority of the female houses in the diocese of Norwich were dedicated to the Virgin Mary, it is not surprising to find that her image dominated their seals. The extant seals display conventions typical of the twelfth century, in particular the 'Throne of Wisdom', in which the Virgin is shown enthroned with the Christ child resting on her knee. The twelfth-century seal of Carrow, for example, portrays the crowned Virgin in profile seated with the Holy Child on her left knee, and a fleur-de-lis, a symbol of the Annunciation, in her right hand. Similarly, the seated Virgin with the Holy Child on her knee decorates a pointed oval twelfth-century seal of Redlingfield Priory in Suffolk.

Monastic seals were a fairly conservative medium. Once established, the image chosen to represent the house was often used for hundreds of years. Hence we find seals dated by documents of the thirteenth and fourteenth centuries retaining stylistic conventions first seen in the twelfth century. A thirteenth-century seal from Carrow is, again, the seated Virgin with the Holy Child. On the left is the prioress kneeling in adoration, holding a scroll bearing the words *Mater D'Meurs*, below a star and crescent moon, which symbolised the chastity of the Virgin. Above the Virgin's head is a hand of blessing. Likewise, a fourteenth-century seal from Campsey Ash is a pointed oval containing the crowned Virgin seated on a throne. In addition to the common seal of a monastery, superiors often possessed their own personal seals. At Bungay, for example, a prioress's seal $c1200$ depicts the familiar image of the enthroned crowned Virgin with the Holy Child on her left knee.

Not infrequently monastic seals portrayed the saints to whom the house was devoted, like the conventual seal of Bungay, which reflected its joint dedication to the Virgin and Holy Cross. Dated by a document of 1360, the seal shows Christ on the Cross with figures kneeling on each side of the base. A similar theme is represented on Flixton's common seal, which is noteworthy given the priory's devotion to the Virgin and St Catherine. This lozenge-shaped seal, dated stylistically to the thirteenth or fourteenth century, depicts Christ on the Cross between St Mary and St John the Evangelist, with the sun and crescent moon. In the base, beneath the arch, is the *Agnus Dei* with symbols of the evangelists. The *Agnus Dei* is the nimbed Lamb of God, which often represented the sacrifice of Christ on the Cross, thus reinforcing the major symbolism of Flixton's seal. The Lamb was also an attribute of St John the Baptist, and in this context its symbolism is combined in a prioress's seal from Bungay, dated $c1300$. It shows John the Baptist with his right hand raised in benediction and his left hand holding a plaque of the *Agnus Dei*; a nun is bowed in prayer at his feet (Plate 1).

These seals from Bungay and Flixton are unique among those of English nunneries in their depiction of Christ on the Cross (Gilchrist 1993), an image which appeared in the late thirteenth century, associated generally with male houses of the mendicant orders (T.A. Heslop pers. com.). This image, combined with the *Agnus Dei*, indicates a strong interest in the Passion and sacrifice of Christ, an interest which informed medieval female piety in the Middle Ages. Such devotion may also have resulted from Bungay's joint dedication to the Holy Cross and the Virgin Mary. Flixton, however, bore no such connection. The symbolism of its seal seems to have been borrowed from that of Bungay, thus reflecting the close geographic proximity of these two houses.

Shared traits were not uncommon among female monastic seals from particular regions, as the round seals of certain Yorkshire nunneries demonstrate. The unusual symbolism shared by Bungay and Flixton may be linked to their status as female houses. In contrast to the seals of male monasteries, the shapes and symbols of which were often determined by membership of a particular monastic order, it seems that social and spiritual bonds among female monasteries determined the symbolism of their seals. Occasionally this imagery was influenced by the precise nature of a monastery's spiritual vocation. A prioress's seal from Crabhouse, appended to a deed dated in the ninth year of the reign of Edward III, for example, is a pointed oval depicting an eagle. The eagle is the symbol of John the Evangelist, to whom the original hermitage and later priory of Crabhouse were both dedicated. This symbolism is apparent in a seal from Hampole, a nunnery in West Yorkshire, which, like Crabhouse, had eremetic associations including an anchoress and a resident hermit.

Plate 1: A prioress's seal from Bungay Priory (Suffolk) dated c1300 shows John the Baptist with his right hand raised in benediction and his left hand holding a plaque of the *Agnus Dei;* a nun is bowed in prayer at his feet. Reproduced with permission of the British Library (seal LXXI.89 9250237).

Because the seals of the female monasteries in East Anglia authenticated business and legal agreements, they reflected a complex web of spiritual symbolism and secular authority. The authority which the seals represented denoted a certain public profile: a visibility which the nunneries' manorial rights and economic privileges guaranteed. More prominent aspects of their material culture, however, were the precincts and buildings in which the nuns lived.

The degree of survival of the archaeological remains of nunneries in Norfolk and Suffolk varies from the well-preserved examples of Carrow and Thetford to the total absence of standing remains at Shouldham and Crabhouse (see Gazetteer). Sources for reconstructing the appearance of the buildings of the cloister include archaeology, architecture, and early illustrations. Martin's *History of Thetford*, for example, shows the priory's buildings *c*1740-50. Documents, particularly medieval household accounts, the inventories of the Dissolution surveyors, and later sixteenth-century property surveys, also provide clues to materials used in constructing monastic buildings. Some indication of materials used at Crabhouse are given in a survey made in 1557 which was executed at the death of the first post-Dissolution owner (Dashwood 1859, 259). The survey distinguished between roofs of slate, reed, or tile, and walls of brick or earth. The composition of the buildings, however, was rarely stated and no distinction was made between buildings of the cloister and those of additional courts. Only one structure was noted for its 'walls of stone', this being 'an old sepale...in breadth square 15' and walls in height 45'.' This description presumably referred to the steeple, or west tower, of the demolished church, as the structure was adjacent to the 'parsons chamber' and 'old churchyard upon the south east' (Figure 3). At least the church was constructed in masonry, fragments of which have been incorporated into Crabbe Abbey house. The main buildings of Crabhouse must have been a combination of flint-rubble, brick and earth construction.

The limited survival of nunnery buildings is due partly to the nature of their original construction, and although we lack details for many of the Norfolk and Suffolk nunneries, equivalent examples from other regions can shed light on their construction (Gilchrist 1993). Certain nunneries in Yorkshire, for example, were recorded at the Dissolution as having been constructed mainly in timber, including Wilberfoss in North Yorkshire. Excavations at Fosse in Lincolnshire have revealed a nunnery constructed in cob. While information about building materials is scarce, reconstructions can be proposed on the basis of surviving earthworks and buildings, evidence from archaeological excavations, cropmarks revealed by aerial photographs, and documents.

Monastic precincts were enclosed by walls, ditches or hedges which acted as legal markers of ownership and served as boundaries between secular and religious worlds. Fragments of flint-rubble precinct walls survive at Bungay,

Monasteries for Women

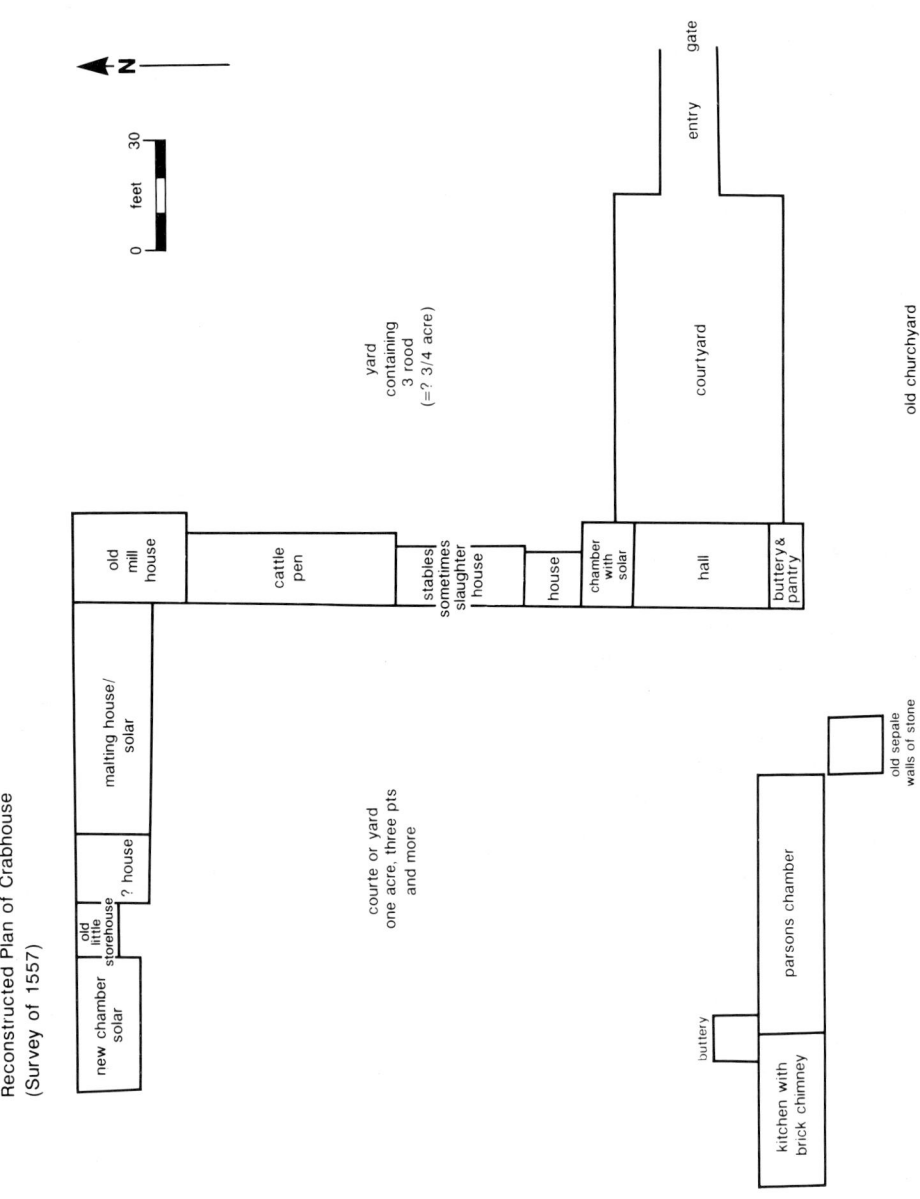

Figure 3: Reconstruction of Crabhouse Priory (Norfolk) based on a survey of 1557.

and walls at Crabhouse were recorded in 1557 as being of brick or earth (Dashwood 1859, 259). Nunneries appear to have been more frequently bounded by moats, traces of which survive at Flixton, Redlingfield, and Bruisyard. The double house at Shouldham was contained within a large precinct defined by ditches. Moats also provided drainage in lowland sites underlain with clay.

In addition to providing a public dividing line and drainage, however, moats served as boundaries with potential symbolic associations. Many post-Conquest nunnery precincts were surrounded by moats which were expensive to build. In this earlier period, such construction signalled a wealthy house with aristocratic affiliations. From the mid-twelfth century, however, when most of the diocese's female houses were built, moat construction was emulated by those of middling social status, the rank of the majority of founders of the monasteries for women in Norfolk and Suffolk. It is possible that certain female houses were moated because they were considered within the wider context of gentry settlement, and thus were perhaps more closely allied to manorial than monastic sites.

Moats and walls defined the outer boundaries of monastic precincts. Inside the precincts, monasteries comprised an outer court for industrial functions, and an inner court for ancillary buildings of the convent. In their outer courts, nunneries would have maintained some industry, storage, and livestock. Inner courts were equipped with bakehouses, brewhouses, and malting houses, although there is little documentary or archaeological evidence for any large scale production, the existence of barns, or extensive storage facilities at the diocese's female houses. Earthwork remains can be discerned for closes and outbuildings at Marham (Plate 2). The Crabhouse cartulary notes a grange, stable, and bakehouse (Bateson 1892, 15); likewise inventories taken at the Dissolution list a bakehouse and brewhouse at Redlingfield and at Campsey Ash (Hazlewood 1894, 15). The absence of excavation in the outer courts of other East Anglian nunneries prevents a full assessment of their functions. Extant structures at Redlingfield and Blackborough, however, indicate that both outer and inner court areas were devoted to domestic residential activity which required well-constructed stone buildings with integral drains. Surviving earthworks and evidence from documents suggest that the outer courts of the Norfolk and Suffolk female houses resembled the majority of English monasteries for women in other dioceses (Gilchrist 1993). Excavations at Elstow in Bedfordshire, for example, revealed that light industry was practised in the outer court, but the presence of hearths and latrines indicated that some structures served a domestic function.

The layout and buildings of a monastic precinct reveal certain aspects of monastic economies. The small precincts and paucity of evidence for light production in the outer court, for example, suggests that the majority of medieval English nunneries were not equipped for self-sufficiency, a

Plate 2: Marham Abbey (Norfolk): earthworks to the south of the church (top left adjacent to the house) represent the cloister and ranges with ancillary buildings to the south. To the north-west of the main cloister (bottom left) is the infirmary cloister. Additional features in the precinct include a number of depressions, which may be fishponds, and a ditched enclosure. Photograph courtesy of Norfolk Landscape Archaeology (TF7009/V/ATZ29).

standard tenet of monasticism. According to the Rule of St Benedict, monasteries should include within their boundaries all things necessary for their sustenance. As we have seen, some of the female houses in the diocese of Norwich possessed water and wind mills, including an extant water mill at Campsey Ash; earthworks indicate possible orchard enclosure at Bruisyard. Evidence for fishponds survives at Campsey Ash, Thetford, Bruisyard, Shouldham and Marham. Blomefield suggested that the fishery at Crabhouse supplied the priory and the local population; few monasteries, however, produced an adequate supply of fish even for internal needs. Indeed, late thirteenth-century cellaress's accounts from Campsey Ash show that the nuns there routinely purchased large quantities of fish. It seems unlikely, therfore, that any of these assets provided the nuns with all that they required. Recent archaeological work at male houses, by contrast, has concentrated on the landscape of the precinct and outer court, revealing thriving areas of light industry, storage of commodities, and management of livestock and fisheries. Such evidence indicates that the male religious were better able to produce enough to supply their own needs.

Evidence of large scale production within the precinct is evident only at Shouldham, where excavations at Abbey Farm uncovered a medieval tile kiln which was used mainly in the production of roof tiles from local sources of clay (Smallwood 1978). In addition to the tile works, aerial photographs indicate that Shouldham maintained an extensive system of fish ponds. The priory's active participation in industrial production was common to double houses elsewhere in England, Nuneaton in Warwickshire, and Stixwould in Lincolnshire, for example, but such activities distinguished it from the other female houses in the diocese.

But were these female houses established with the goal of self-sufficiency in mind? We have already seen that the geographic settings and small endowments of these convents were not necessarily a comment by patrons on the lesser value of female than male religious, but rather reflected assumptions regarding the functions of monasteries for women. It is possible that if the nuns' piety and spirituality were highly valued by their secular neighbours, economic support could be anticipated through the benefactions of local people. As the following chapters show, this support was indeed forthcoming and continued throughout the Middle Ages, thus suggesting that monasteries for women may never have been intended to be economically self-supporting.

While many monasteries diverted water courses in order to have fresh water for kitchens and channels to flush latrines, female houses seldom possessed elaborate facilities. At Crabhouse the water source for the house (the 'lode', possibly from *l'eau*) ran through 'le clos de la curt' (Bateson 1892, 9), apparently an open water course rather than a conduit. In contrast to the provision at male houses, such as Castle Acre, few female houses were equipped with latrines flushed by running water (*reredorters*). Indeed, excavations at Higham in Kent, and at Denny in Cambridgeshire, have revealed ordinary garderobes more akin to secular manorial sites. Most convents were provided with small L-shaped structures adjacent to the dormitory over the east range. Foundations of such a structure to the east of

Carrow's dormitory range have been attributed with this function, although its position near the chapter-house is unusual – a more discrete situation towards the south of the range was normally preferred (Figure 5).

Monastic kitchens can occasionally be located in relation to a likely water source. Kitchens seldom survive, however, given that they were detached from the cloister and often of insubstantial construction. At Thetford it has been suggested that a well was positioned near the south range, where a kitchen would be expected. The extant buildings at Redlingfield and Blackborough suggest possible sites of monastic kitchens. At Redlingfield a rectangular structure of flint-rubble retains two pointed arched openings at the base of its north wall, possibly relating to a conduit for a kitchen or ancillary domestic structure (Plate 3). A similar feature occurs in a partially extant structure at Blackborough which is also of relatively high quality construction (see Gazetteer). These buildings seem to have been equipped with drains to serve either kitchens or latrines, thus confirming the domestic function observed elsewhere for the outer courts of monasteries for women.

A nunnery's inner court often provided housing for the diverse lay residents which most monasteries accommodated. In 1414, for example, Flixton Priory housed at least sixteen corrodians, two chaplains, and twenty hinds and household servants within the priory's precincts (SRO, HA/12/B2-/18/14). Such living arrangements in these small convents were flexible, as shown in the reconstruction plan of Crabhouse based on the 1557 survey (Figure 3). Two courts or yards are indicated in relation to the 'hall', the original west range of the convent. The first court, to the north of the cloister, faced onto the mill house, cattle pen, stables and refectory. The second court, to the west of the 'hall', was 'inclosed about with howses and bricke walls, and the other parte with erth walle,' and contained the malting house, storehouses, and the parson's chamber. This last structure was adjacent to the west tower of the conventual church. The western siting of the outer court allowed the laity entry to the nuns' church through the west door without ingress to their cloister.

The highest quality accommodation was often in the nunneries' guest houses, forming the west range of the cloister, but facing onto the inner court. Visitors' quarters were generally sited in the west range, which was sometimes shared with the prioress's lodgings, as indicated by extant ranges at Polsloe near Exeter, and at Kington St Michael in Wiltshire. This arrangement is suggested at Crabhouse, where documents reveal a west

Monasteries for Women

Plate 3: Redlingfield Priory (Suffolk): north gable of a monastic building, currently in use as a farm building. The two blocked arched openings at its base may have related to a conduit.

Plate 4: St Andrew's parish church, Redlingfield (Suffolk) with a monastic building sited $c36$ metres to the south. The nuns shared the church with the parish. The building in the foreground may have been sited in the inner court, possibly as accommodation for guests or lay people living in the precinct.

range hall with the prioress's chamber at the upper end, and at Carrow, where the extant range was divided between a hall and prioress's lodging, which was fully rebuilt in the sixteenth century (Plate 5) (see Gazetteer). At Marham, a portion of the west range survives. This vaulted chamber contains the only fragment of figurative sculpture to survive *in situ* at any of the diocese's female houses. In the south-east corner the ribs of the vaulting are supported by a half-figure of a bearded knight, a representation more likely to occur in the secular context of the guest accommodations (Figure 4). East Anglian prioresses are known to have maintained their own chambers in the west range, but, in contrast to their male counterparts, did not build detached lodgings.

Plate 5: Carrow Priory, Norwich c1932-9: the site of the priory is in the centre of the photograph, consisting of the ruined church and east range and the medieval portion of the standing building in the background. The sixteenth-century prioress's lodge is contained in the eastern (right) section of the standing building, with the site of the cloister to its east. The complete foundations of the conventual church are visible to the right (north), where Colman's works canteen now stands.

While the inner court housed secular guests, additional local lay people commonly worshipped in the conventual church. Even where a parish church was situated close by, as at Marham and Carrow, for example, parishioners often requested burial in the convent's churchyard. The sharing of conventual churches sometimes led to an unorthodox (reversal) of the choir from the east to west end, as at Marrick in North Yorkshire, or to the construction

Figure 4: A corbel supporting the vaulting at the north end of the west range at Marham (Norfolk). The ribs are supported by a half-figure of a bearded knight with a gauntlet or sword-hilt (illustration by Ted West).

of two parallel aisles: one for the nuns, the other for parishioners, such as Ickleton in Cambridgeshire. In Norfolk and Suffolk, the portion of the church designated for the laity seems to have been confined to the nave, west of the crossing or *pulpitum*. This arrangement was certainly the case at Bungay (Plate 6), Thetford, and Redlingfield, and is suggested at Crabhouse.

The conventual churches of nunneries were generally aisleless parallelograms with a screen dividing the nave from the choir and presbytery, as the remains from Marham (Plate 7) and Redlingfield indicate

Plate 6: Bungay Priory (Suffolk): remains of the nuns' choir (foreground) are located east of the chancel of the aisled parish church. The nuns' cloister was north of their ruined church.

(Plate 4). Cruciform churches survive at Carrow, Thetford, and Bungay, which may reflect the origins and functions of these particular houses (Figure 5). Recall that Thetford began as a cell of monks from Bury St Edmunds; Carrow was a royal foundation; and Bungay served the needs of a market town. Excavations at Campsey Ash, the wealthiest nunnery in the diocese, indicated an unaisled choir containing a private burial chapel (see Gazetteer), although a plan of the remains in 1790 suggested an unaisled nave (Nichols 1790, vol. 5, no. 5). Aerial photographs of Shouldham have revealed cropmarks which suggest an elaborate cruciform church terminating

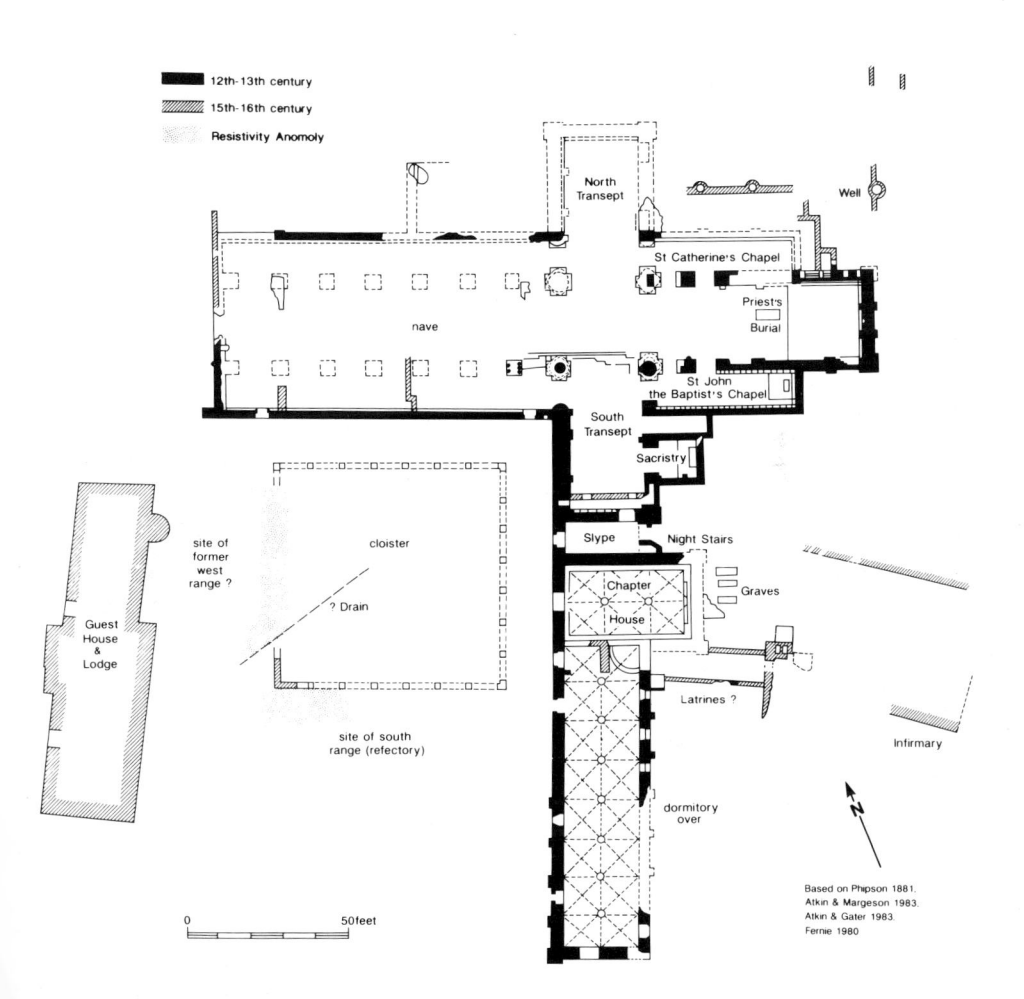

Figure 5: Carrow Priory (Norfolk): a composite plan based on standing remains, excavation and resistivity survey.

in three eastern chapels with the cloister to the north (Plate 9). On the basis of analogy with the excavated Gilbertine house at Watton (Humberside), provision at Shouldham would have included two separate and detached cloisters for the nuns and canons. The main conventual church would have adjoined the nuns' cloister, and would have been divided longitudinally in order to provide separate aisles which ensured sexual segregation. The canons would have been provided with an additional smaller chapel for their own regular use. The cropmarks represent robber-trenches of the foundations of the main conventual church at Shouldham, with the nuns' cloister to the north.

The nucleus of all monastic precincts was the cloister around which the monastic ranges were grouped. The space of the cloister was flanked by walkways which ran concentrically and provided access to three ranges and the church. While most monasteries were provided with freestanding cloisters supported on an arcade, many female houses formed a courtyard through the use of a pentice construction, as at Aconbury in Herefordshire. This was a corridor with a single-pitch roof which ran along the side of the building and was carried on corbels. At Marham and Campsey Ash evidence survives for a pentice against the wall of the church and west range, respectively (Plates 7 and 10). This less substantial construction may account for the relatively poor survival of monastic architecture for women, and certainly comments on the accommodation deemed appropriate for nuns.

Cloisters generally adjoined their churches to the south in the standard Benedictine fashion (Figure 5). East Anglian convents with south cloisters include Carrow, Thetford, Redlingfield, Campsey Ash, and Marham. Some female houses, however, built their cloisters to the north of the church, as at Bungay, Shouldham and Crabhouse. These exceptions form part of a wider national pattern in which approximately thirty-three per cent of female houses were built with north cloisters. This northern orientation was an aspect of architectural iconography and not a product of topographical restrictions (Gilchrist 1992). North cloister nunneries seem to have been built in reference to an earlier tradition in which women and female saints were associated with the northern parts of churches. This tradition encompassed a series of overlapping associations with women, including early medieval sexual segregation in church worship, iconographies of the Virgin Mary which emphasised her place at the Crucifixion and her Coronation, and the attendance of the Holy Women at the Sepulchre.

Plate 7: Marham Abbey (Norfolk): remains of the south wall of the church, with two circular windows, and the north end of the west range. Earthworks to the south represent the monastic cloister with ancillary buildings or inner court beyond (adjacent to the refectory). Photograph courtesy of Norfolk Landscape Archaeology (TF7009/S/ATZ26).

Plate 8: Thetford Priory (Norfolk): remains of the chapter-house (right, formerly part of the east range) and the exterior of the south transept of the nuns' church. The rough outer face of the transept is where the east range would have joined. The square, projecting south-east corner turret housed night-stairs into the church from the dormitory over the east range.

Monasteries for Women

Plate 9: Site of Shouldham Priory (Norfolk): cropmarks represent the robber-trenches of the foundations of the north transept and east end of the church, with three chapels, and claustral buildings to the north. Photograph courtesy of Norfolk Landscape Archaeology (DJY9).

Plate 10: Campsey Ash Priory (Suffolk): the west range of the nunnery has been converted to a farm building. It retains a blocked thirteenth-century doorway and stone moulding indicating the line of the pentice roof of the west cloister walk.

In common with nunneries in other regions, the East Anglian group exhibits a degree of unorthodox cloister orientation, with at least three north cloisters identified. For the most part, the layout and buildings of many of the country's monasteries for women, the East Anglian ones included, incorporated a number of features more characteristic of manorial than mainstream monastic settlement, and share in a national pattern of female monastic sites. The use of the moat to define the precinct area, for example, is more indicative of manorial and lesser monasteries which often functioned as granges, such as smaller alien priories and preceptories. Likewise, the courtyard format adopted by the Norfolk and Suffolk convents, as well as female houses elsewhere, was equally at home in later manorial complexes, particularly where this layout was facilitated by a pentice in preference to the construction of a cloister, as at Campsey Ash and Marham. The west ranges of many female houses, like those at Carrow, Crabhouse, and Marham, were often ordered as secular halls, with a central hall divided from an upper and lower end. West ranges commonly benefited from a significant portion of a monastery's resources which is reflected in the quality of the buildings which survive.

Why should the material culture of these and other monasteries for women take their cue from manorial secular architecture? The answer lies in the social status of many of the houses' founders, the social ranks from which most nuns came, and the types of patronage the nuns garnered. These aspects combined to place monasteries for women in the broader setting of later medieval gentry society and are discussed more fully in the following chapters.

Chapter 3
The Nuns of Norfolk and Suffolk

Medieval English nuns represented a small percentage of the total female population. Historians estimate that before the outbreak of the plague in 1349, there were roughly 5,000 nuns in England. Their numbers fell by about one-third in the following fifty years, but by the middle of the fifteenth century, the female monastic population began a slow but steady recovery. The number of nuns never reached the pre-plague figure, however, and by the time of the Dissolution of the monasteries there were less than 2000 nuns in England (Power 1922, 3; Russell 1944, 179-85).

The female monastic population of the diocese of Norwich comprised about one-fifth of the country's total population of nuns, and sustained similar losses as a result of the plague. Although precise figures are impossible to obtain, we can estimate that between the years 1150 and 1349, around 1,500 nuns lived in the diocese's eleven convents. Between 1350 and 1400, the number of nuns dropped to about 300. Their numbers increased slowly throughout the fifteenth century, and between 1400 and 1540, nearly 900 nuns lived in the counties of Norfolk and Suffolk (Oliva 1994, forthcoming).

This chapter examines several aspects of the diocese's nuns, including the social groups and geographic regions from which they came, and the nature of their lives in the cloister. While their daily routine revolved around the recitation of the canonical services known as the Divine Office, this chapter will show that most of the nuns also participated in a variety of other activities. In addition to communal and individual reading and prayer, most nuns participated in the management of their convents. Some of their administrative duties brought them into contact with the secular world. Despite the nuns' more worldly concerns and activities, however, they maintained a high standard of religious life.

The Nuns of Norfolk and Suffolk

A prosopographical study, or group biography, of the nuns was carried out to determine the social ranks of the diocese's female monastic population. Using wills, heraldic visitations, pedigrees, and the Inquisitions Post Mortem, 572 nuns who lived in Norfolk and Suffolk between 1350 and the Dissolution can be identified by name. These sources also yielded data about the family backgrounds and social ranks of 250 of these 572 identifiable nuns. This biographical analysis concludes that the majority of the nuns of the Norwich diocese came from families of the middling ranks of society, at least sixty-four per cent (Oliva 1990), and not from the social elite, as historians have previously maintained (Knowles 1959, 75; Power 1922, 42, 76, 95).

This study of the social status of the nuns is weighted toward the later Middle Ages because our sources of information are much more plentiful for this later period. Though a smattering of wills dated before 1350 are extant, and the Inquisitions Post Mortem are also available for an earlier period, they do not contain information about the social ranks of these religious women before 1350. Nevertheless, the convents' sizes and economic status suggest that the findings for the social background of later medieval nuns also represent the backgrounds of earlier nuns.

The nuns can be classified into five social categories. The highest was the aristocracy, which included royal women, those who came from families with hereditary peerage titles, and those from county families of national status and prestige. This social group enjoyed the wealth and privilege that accompanied lordship over vast estates, as well as the responsibilities of being the Crown's chief counsellors in the House of Lords. Two of the East Anglian nuns fall into this category, Katherine Beauchamp and Countess Maud of Ulster and Oxford; but they were part of a tiny percentage of nuns who came from this social group. Only seven of the 572 identifiable nuns who lived in the diocese from 1350 to 1540 belonged to this top level of society.

Directly below the aristocracy in social rank were nuns from the families of the upper gentry. While they shared certain characteristics with the titled aristocracy, in particular the dependence for wealth and power on landed estates and agricultural production, and involvement with the affairs of the realm as well as with those of the counties from which they came or wherein they held their titles, nevertheless, the upper gentry formed a distinct second social group. Nuns in this category came from families whose fathers and brothers were knights and esquires, were elected to the House of Commons, or filled county offices such as sheriff and escheator. Katherine Clifton fits into this group, a Cistercian nun at Marham Abbey in 1367 and a daughter of Sir Adam Clifton, Knight, Lord of Topcroft Manor and lands elsewhere in Norfolk. So does Dorothy Calthorp, a sixteenth-century nun at Bruisyard Abbey. She was the daughter of Sir Philip Calthorp, Knight and Sheriff of Norfolk in 1489/90. Overall, only about fifteen per cent of the diocese's nuns came from upper gentry families such as these.

The third social group was the lower gentry, or what some historians call the parish gentry. Although they were sometimes cadet branches of upper gentry families, the parish gentry were less well-propertied. They further differed from the upper gentry in their involvement with local parish and village affairs, by holding minor offices like constable and bailiff, and by serving as stewards for more prestigious families. The last prioress of Crabhouse, Elizabeth Studefield, and her brother Sebastian who was the priory's bailiff, belonged to this middling social rank. So did Katherine Simonds, refectress and then second prioress of Campsey Ash. This social group contributed by far the largest number of nuns to the diocese's female houses: sixty-four per cent. Women from the parish gentry thus contrasted greatly with those of the titled aristocracy and the upper gentry in terms of their general representation as a population group resident within these convents.

Urban dwellers represented the fourth social group, who can be distinguished from the titled aristocracy and the upper gentry by their urban residence, involvement with trade and industry, and interests in civic government. This group included nuns like Margaret Folcard, only daughter of John Folcard, citizen and alderman of Norwich, who was at Carrow Priory in the 1460s, and Alice Cook, a nun at Campsey Ash in the sixteenth century. Her father was John Cook, draper, who also served as alderman, sheriff and mayor of Norwich in the late fifteenth century. The number of nuns from this social group in the female houses was slightly higher than the number of nuns from the upper gentry and considerably lower than the number of nuns from the parish gentry, as they comprised sixteen per cent of all the identifiable nuns. Most of the nuns from urban families went to Carrow Priory which was located outside the town walls of the city of Norwich. As Norwich was the main urban centre of the diocese, geographical proximity of the families to this convent probably played a significant part in attracting nuns from urban families to this house.

Similar in wealth and local interests to the parish gentry was the fifth social rank: substantial freeholders, or yeoman farmers, a social group more difficult to identify than the other groups discussed here. The yeomen generally did not hold any local offices and had no pretense to gentility - that intangible quality often used to distinguish the gentry from lower social ranks. Alice Fermer, a nun at Thetford Priory in the early sixteenth century, was from a family who falls into this fifth category of social rank. Her father left her a brass pot in his will, one of the few things he had to bequeath to his heirs (NRO, ANF 188 Shaw). At least four per cent of all the identifiable nuns in the diocese were of this social group.

As these examples demonstrate, the vast majority of rank and file nuns were from the parish gentry. The predominance of nuns from middling social ranks was also true, moreover, of the monasteries' abbesses and prioresses. Five of the prioresses at the time of the Dissolution left wills which provide clues about their social backgrounds. These monastic superiors were clearly not from the upper end of the social scale. Their bequests were insubstantial, consisting of personal belongings, including beds, bedding, and clothing, and while they bequeathed a few silver spoons and a bit of money, they did not have any superfluous items to pass on. Grace Sampson, ex-prioress of Redlingfield, had just two silver goblets, a dozen silver spoons (items purchased from the priory from which she was expelled), and some money to leave to friends (NRO, NCC 235 Bircham). The last prioress of Campsey Ash, Ela Buttery, left only a few pairs of sheets and three marks (NRO, NCC 261 Hyll). Her poverty was reflected in the manner chosen to mark her grave. Her funerary brass, which survives in St Stephen's church, Norwich, was an earlier brass appropriated for her use in 1546 (Manning 1864, 296).

The legatees of the ex-prioress's wills also indicate women from the middle ranks of medieval society. Barbara Mason, the last abbess of Marham, was the only superior to mention siblings; and they are untraceable in the sources which provide evidence for the upper levels of society. Cecil Fastolf, the last prioress of Bungay, remembered two nieces; Grace Sampson left everything she owned to the Bedingfields, the family who acquired the priory over which she was prioress. Ela Buttery bequeathed her few personal belongings to fellow ex-nuns of Campsey Ash. If these nuns had been from upper gentry families, they would have returned to them after the Dissolution, as did nuns in other parts of England (see Chapter 5).

This distribution of social ranks in the female houses was consistent with their small sizes and relative poverty. Most of the convents, while accommodating a handful of upper gentry nuns, were overwhelmingly populated by women from the parish gentry and urban families. Only Campsey Ash, the wealthiest house in the diocese, attracted a significant number of upper gentry nuns. The evidence for the social status of these medieval nuns thus indicates a far more diverse female monastic population than has been previously realised.

In addition to providing evidence about the nuns' social and family backgrounds, the prosopographical analysis yields information about the geographic regions from which the nuns came. Of the 572 identifiable nuns, the geographic origins of 106 can be determined from wills, records from Inquisitions Post Mortem, heraldic visitations, and pedigrees. These sources indicate that about eighteen per cent of the identifiable nuns came from within a ten to fifteen mile radius of the religious houses which they entered. Anne King, for example, was a nun at Bungay Priory from at least 1520 until the Dissolution in 1536. We know that she was from the town of Bungay because her father, Robert Wingfield, says so in his will of 1523 (NRO, NCC 181-182 Albaster). Similarly, Jane Dereham, a sixteenth-century nun of Crabhouse, was the daughter of Thomas Dereham of Crimplesham, Norfolk, and his wife Isabel. Jane, then, was also a recruit who lived close to the convent she entered (Rye 1891 vol. 23, 105).

The nuns who lived in the eleven monasteries for women in the diocese of Norwich were drawn primarily from local families. The evidence for nuns elsewhere in England, and monks and canons in the diocese of Norwich, suggests a similar pattern of local recruits of middling social status. John Tillotson found that the nuns at Marrick Priory in Yorkshire were from local families of middling social rank (Tillotson 1989, 6). And both H.G.D. Liveing and H. F. Chettle described the novices of Romsey and Barking Abbeys as county 'gentle folk' and 'tradesmen's daughters,' suggesting similar backgrounds for the nuns of these prominent houses in Hampshire and Essex, respectively (Liveing 1906, 113; Chettle 1954, 54). Both the Cathedral Priory and the friaries in the city of Norwich recruited from local and suburban families (Tanner 1984, 25-6); the Carmelite friars of Ipswich came primarily from local Suffolk villages (Redstone 1898-1900, 193). The canons of Butley Priory and Leiston Abbey were also mostly from the vicinity of these two male houses (Mortimer 1979, 8).

As we shall see, the predominance of local recruits enhanced relations between the female houses in the diocese of Norwich with their neighbours (see Chapter 4). Similar relationships between other religious institutions which recruited locally and their immediate neighbours have been identified by Norman Tanner in his survey of testamentary bequests in the diocese of Norwich in the later Middle Ages (Tanner 1984, 119-129).

Regardless of their social background, monastic recruits had to meet certain qualifications in order to be accepted into a religious house. They had to be legitimately born and be physically and mentally fit for the rigours of a monastic life. They were also expected to have attained a certain degree of education, or demonstrate the ability to learn how to read the Latin prayers of the Divine Office.

Several perceptions exist about medieval nuns, including the age of entry into a convent and the motives a woman had when entering a religious house. Many historians maintain that social and economic circumstances forced families to dump infants, undowerable daughters, and burdensome, aged widows into female monasteries, with little concern for their religious vocations (Power 1922, 25-6; Shahar 1983, 39). Evidence about the nuns of Norfolk and Suffolk suggests that these generalisations are inaccurate. There are only a handful of cases in the diocese of Norwich of either very young girls or widows entering a house as a novice. Guy Beauchamp, Earl of Warwick, enlisted his two daughters, Katherine and Margaret, aged seven and one respectively, in Shouldham Priory (*VCH, Norfolk* vol. 2, 413), and Maud of Ulster became a nun at Campsey Ash after the death of her second husband, Ralph of Ufford (*CPL* vol. 4, 37). But most of the women who became nuns in the diocese were between fourteen and seventeen years of age, and appear to have become nuns not because of family pressure, but rather because they had genuine religious vocations (Oliva 1994, forthcoming).

Another common misconception about female monasteries is that they demanded hefty doweries from the families of recruits (Power 1922, 19-24). A few women in the diocese were bequeathed substantial sums of money if they became nuns. John Castleacre, for example, left his daughter Mary £10 to become a nun at Marham (NRO, NCC 152-53 Surflete). But there is no evidence to suggest that the female monasteries in the diocese of Norwich many of their male counterparts throughout the later Middle Ages (Oliva 1994, forthcoming).

The nuns' efficient running of their households undoubtedly contributed to the high standard of religious life which they maintained. Problems which mismanagement and debt caused in other female and male houses, such as disregard for the daily office, non-observance of saints' days, or improper dress, for example, (Jessopp 1888, 6, 54, 76, 96; Power 1922, *passim*), did not plague the female monasteries in the diocese of Norwich. With the exception of Redlingfield, which suffered some scandal in the early fifteenth century under the unsteady stewardship of Prioress Isabella Hermit (Thompson 1915-1927 vol. 3, 415), the late fifteenth- and sixteenth-century bishops' visitations record only isolated and minor incidences of deviation from the monastic rule. The most serious problem occurred at Crabhouse where one of the nuns was relegated to the lowest end of the seating at the refectory table for having born a child (Jessopp 1888, 108-10). Less serious infringements happened at Carrow where in 1532, some of the younger nuns were cautioned against wearing silk waist-bands and gossiping (Jessopp 1888, 274). The majority of complaints about the nuns in the diocese, however, concerned the amount of food and the strength of the ale they received (Jessopp 1888, *passim*).

The standard of religious life which is thus reflected in the episcopal visitation records indicates that the nuns in the diocese held genuine vocations which they followed in community with others. Their piety is perhaps best reflected, however, in the amount of patronage that they attracted from lay society. This patronage was especially forthcoming from the social groups from which the majority of nuns came and with whom they had the most contact, the parish gentry and yeoman farmers.

Chapter 4
Piety and Patronage

From the Crown, to bishops, to members of the local gentry, people from all levels of medieval society patronised the female houses in the diocese of Norwich with a range of grants and favours. Repeating an earlier decree, for example, Pope Sixtus IV granted to the nuns of Bruisyard and all others associated with the abbey, an indulgence which included choice of confessor and plenary remission of sin, regardless of their proximity to the abbey, at the hour of death (*CPL* vol. 13:2, 646-47). The cruciform plan and impressive size of the church of Carrow, which was larger than any other parish or monastic church in Norwich with the exception of the Cathedral Priory, reflected the initial royal patronage which the priory received, rather than the requirement of a convent of twelve nuns. Bishop Broun left 13*s*. 4*d*. to the prioress of Redlingfield, 3*s*. 4*d*. to each nun there, and fifteen marks to the convent for the purchase of a Sarum grail. He made similar bequests to the nuns of Carrow and Flixton (Jacob 1965, 436). Both Bruisyard Abbey and Bungay Priory benefited from the largesse of the Countess of Suffolk who boarded her daughters at each house (BL, Egerton Roll 8776).

The patronage that the female houses drew from all levels of society corresponded to the spiritual and temporal activities in which the nuns engaged, activities which reflected the dual nature of their vocations. A nun's vocation comprised in equal degrees the contemplative nature of Mary and the active nature of Martha, qualities which, if ably demonstrated, guaranteed the support of medieval secular society.

This chapter examines this reciprocity of piety and patronage by surveying the spiritual and temporal activities of the nuns and the ways in which the lay community responded to their actions. A correspondence will be demonstrated between socially elite groups and certain monasteries for women: a correlation which was limited, however, to the fourteenth century. A more consistent pattern of patronage established a stronger connection

Bungay the nuns allotted at least 2*s*. to the poor on the anniversary of their foundress's death (*VE* vol. 3, 431); the prioress there distributed the larger sum of 12*s*. 8*d*. on the same day (SRO, HD 1538/345). Blackborough, Crabhouse, and Redlingfield made similar donations in food and money to the poor at specified times throughout the year (Oliva 1994, forthcoming).

While their small size and relative poverty rendered them less able to give abundantly than their wealthier male counterparts, the nuns appear to have executed their eleemosynary duties very effectively. The nuns at Blackborough Priory, for example, spent at least seven per cent of their revenues on alms for the poor; Redlingfield contributed approximately thirteen per cent annually for alms; and Bruisyard dispersed a full seventeen per cent of their income a year to the poor (Oliva 1994, forthcoming). These percentages are significant when seen in the context of the convents' annual incomes. Blackborough's yearly revenues, for example, totalled about £42; Redlingfield's income was only £67, while Bruisyard had only £56 a year to manage (Table 1). The percentages which these houses spent on alms to the poor constituted a considerable proportion of these monastic budgets.

The amount of money spent on alms by male houses in the diocese was considerably less. The average contribution made by the monks and canons to the poor and needy was between three and five per cent of their yearly revenues (Knowles 1959 vol. 3, 264-265; Savine 1909, 236-37). The monks at St Benedict at Hulme, for example, distributed £5 a year in alms for the poor: less than five per cent of their annual income of £583. The canons at Sibton Abbey in Suffolk gave even less, although their doles increased in the sixteenth century at the behest of the bishop (Denny 1960 vol. 1, 27, 30).

Not all of the diocese's male houses spent so little. Bury St Edmunds, the priory at Eye, and the monks at Ixworth all contributed substantial amounts of their yearly budgets to the poor in alms (*VCH, Suffolk* vol. 2, 68-69, 73, 105). The generosity of these houses, however, stands in stark contrast not only to the smaller amounts donated by the majority of the other male houses, but also to the larger problem of alms-abuse, a problem which characterised the male monasteries throughout the Middle Ages (Cheney 1936, 112; Jessopp 1888, 215, 279).

Interestingly, there is no evidence to indicate that the nuns diverted any of the money earmarked for alms, food scraps, or articles of clothing from the poor and needy. The nuns' proper administration of money, food and clothes to the poor suggests a gender-related difference between the female houses and their male counterparts. Is it possible that as women, traditionally seen as care-takers and nurturers, the nuns took these charitable responsibilities more seriously than the monks and canons? In any case, the nuns' greater attention to the poor no doubt enhanced their local reputations which in turn elicited support from their neighbours.

More temporal activities in which the nuns engaged, and for which they were rewarded, included providing hospitality to the people known as corrodians: life-time residents who received room and board from the nuns in exchange for a sum of money or parcel of land. Several of the diocese's houses accommodated corrodians throughout the Middle Ages. In 1414, for example, fifteen corrodians were resident at Flixton Priory including two unnamed brothers, their wives and two maids; three sisters, their maid and chaplain; Roger Hord and his wife Pamela; a man named Blynde and his wife; and a Margaret Broton (SRO, HA/12/B2/18/14). Two married couples were corrodians at Crabhouse in the mid-fourteenth century; and Marham supported three corrodians in 1468 (Bateson 1892, 42-43; NRO, Hare 2208 194x5).

In addition to corrodians, other people used the female houses as places of retreat. Such visitors included those who visited the convents for extended periods of time, like the Countess of Suffolk's daughters. The beleaguered lovers Richard Calle and Margery Paston stayed for a time at Blackborough until the Pastons came to accept this unwelcome match (Oliva 1994, forthcoming). No less than 250 boarders stayed at Carrow Priory from the late fourteenth century through the mid-fifteenth. These people varied in social status from a single woman, Alice de Cheselden, to more illustrious people like Lady Margaret Kerdeston, her servant, and her daughter (Rye 1889, 48-52).

Like Carrow, the other female monasteries in the diocese accommodated a socially mixed group of temporary visitors. The nuns at Bungay, for example, boarded Margaret Alman for a year in 1512 (SRO, HD 1538/156/17). At Marham, the daughter of Edmund Berry, Knight, coincided with the six-month stay of a man named Leonard Cotton (NRO, Hare 2205 194x5). The nuns at Redlingfield welcomed Lady Katherine Boteler, a woman named Alice Charles, and unnamed others throughout the fifteenth century (SRO, HD 1538/327). The female houses were popular retreats for people from all levels of medieval Norfolk and Suffolk society. Did these lay visitors financially burden, over-crowd, or distract the nuns from their contemplative duties of prayer and meditation, and thus compromise their piety, as historians have previously suggested (Coulton 1930, 51; Knowles 1959 vol. 3, 260-262; Snape 1926, 14-19)? Apparently not. Evidence for the expenses incurred by these boarders shows that, in general, they did not impose great financial stress on the nuns. Household accounts survive for Bungay, Carrow, Marham, and Redlingfield which show that the nuns at these convents received sufficient funds from their boarders to off-set the costs of their hospitality (Oliva 1994, forthcoming). In addition to this direct evidence, these houses did not suffer from chronic debt, in contrast to many of the male houses, whose numerous lay visitors contributed significantly to the debt incurred by the monks and canons throughout the period, despite their larger holdings and substantially higher revenues. St Benedict at Hulme, Creake and Langley Abbeys, Wymondham and Bromholm Priories, Norwich Cathedral Priory, Horsham St Faith and Beeston are just a few of the male houses which struggled with debt in the later Middle Ages, in part because of the number of guests and servants they maintained (Oliva 1994, forthcoming).

Despite their smaller foundations and incomes, the female houses employed enough household servants to attend to the needs of their long- and short-term visitors throughout the Middle Ages. With some fluctuations over time, and some variations from house to house, the monasteries for women retained fairly stable populations of household servants and guests to nuns: an average ratio of two to one, a servant and lodger to each nun. The cellaress and superior were responsible for estimating costs and paying for the food necessary to accommodate their guests, and the nuns employed enough household servants to free themselves from the day-to-day responsibilities for their secular guests (Oliva 1994, forthcoming). Several of the nuns' guests even brought their own maids with them, surely lessening the burden of their stays.

While we have drawn primarily from wills to demonstrate the value of the nuns to lay society, entries in the convents' extant household accounts confirm that lay people supported the nuns for the activities described above. In her account of 1490/91, Elizabeth Stevenson, prioress of Bungay, noted that 4*s*. were received in offerings to the convents placed before the Holy Cross in the priory church (SRO, HD 1538/156/14). In 1512/13, the same prioress received 6*s*. 8*d*. in alms from William Marchaunt, chaplain, to repair the watermill in Wangford (SRO, HD 1538/156/17). Margery Harsyk, the abbess of Marham, received '30*s*. in diverse alms....and 6*s*. 8*d*. from Thomas Wesenham as a gift' in 1405/06 (NRO, Hare 2201 194x5). In her account dated 1419/20, Harsyk entered receipts totalling 77*s*. 8*d*. from alms given to the abbey (NRO, Hare 2204 194x5).

A monastery's reputation spread far and wide. In consequence complaints about male houses may explain the nuns' greater popularity with local testators, and the more substantial patronage which they showed to the nuns throughout the Middle Ages. Although smaller and poorer than their male counterparts, the nuns' contributions to lay society seem nevertheless to have had a more positive impact. Their strength of piety and sincerity of vocation were demonstrated in all of their spiritual and temporal activities, activities which earned the continued support of secular society.

While the nuns enjoyed the gifts and favours of secular society, they were not the only female religious in the diocese of Norwich to do so. Many other religious women led lives of religious dedication who were equally valued by lay people around them. It is to these other holy women that we must now turn in order to see the broader landscape of female piety in medieval East Anglia.

Chapter 5
Hospitals, Informal Communities, and Individual Ascetics

Religious life for medieval women in East Anglia embraced a number of options. As described in Chapter 1, both communal and individual lifestyles offered women a variety of paths to follow. If the cloister was too confining, one could opt for another kind of vocation sanctioned by the Church, the life of a hospital sister. For a woman whose vocation dictated a more solitary existence, the life of an anchoress, hermit, or vowess provided a more extreme religious life. Still other women in East Anglia created their own religious lifestyles which appear to have been more fluid and less restrictive than those regulated by the Church. While the previous chapters of this survey have focused on life in monasteries for women, this chapter examines the other options, including community-based religious life and individual religious vocations. A survey of these other religious lifestyles reveals certain aspects of medieval female piety. First, the variety of religious lifestyles that we have identified in the diocese of Norwich demonstrates that the opportunities for spiritual life for medieval women were far greater than previously supposed (Devlin 1984, 183). Second, the continuous presence of both groups and individual religious women in certain parts of medieval East Anglia indicates a lasting tradition which was fostered throughout the period by local lay people and male clerics. Finally, each of the options discussed here broadens our understanding of female piety, allowing us to place these religious communities and individual ascetics into the wider context of medieval female spirituality.

A nun enjoyed a dual vocation, one which reflected the contemplative nature of Mary and the more active life of Martha. For a woman whose vocation was oriented toward greater participation in the world, the life of a hospital sister was perhaps more fitting than the life of a cloistered nun. Medieval hospitals served the poor, the aged, the sick, and sometimes

Hospitals, Informal Communities, and Individual Ascetics

travellers in need of temporary lodging (Cullum 1991). Knowles and Hadcock identified ninety hospitals in the diocese of Norwich (Knowles and Hadcock 1971). This figure represents the minimum number likely to have existed in the diocese; additional examples are being uncovered by current research on medieval hospitals (Carole Rawcliffe pers. com.). Of these ninety, at least fourteen had sisters among staff and inmates (Table 2). Carbrooke was staffed by women until at least 1180, after which many of the sisters of this hospital of the Order of St John of Jerusalem were transferred to Minchin Buckland, a double monastery of the Hospitallers in Somerset. Eleven of the diocese's hospitals were run strictly by men; the available sources prohibit us from knowing which of the remaining minimum number of sixty-six hospitals were for women, men, or both. It is probable, therefore, that more hospitals maintained a female staff than the fourteen identified to date.

Of the fourteen known hospitals which included women among their staff, four were established in Suffolk; the rest were in Norfolk. At least two hospitals for women were founded in Bury St Edmunds and the city of Norwich. Eleven of the hospitals fell in the sweep of suppressions in the 1530s and 1540s. Only two, St Mary Magdalen in Beccles, and the hospital of St James and the Trinity in Dunwich, survived and continued to serve as almshouses for women through the seventeenth century.

Like medieval monasteries, hospitals were dedicated to particular patron saints (Table 2). While sharing similar saints' dedications with the female houses, hospitals were more commonly devoted to Mary Magdalen, like those in Beccles and King's Lynn. She was associated with healing through a conflation of biblical episodes, including her links with the house of Simon the leper, the illness of Lazarus, and her anointing of the feet of Christ. Her special place at the Resurrection further contributed to this connection with healing.

Certain other saints were more popular with hospitals than monasteries, particularly the hospitals associated with pilgrims. St James was the patron saint of the hospital in Dunwich, for example; and St Giles was the saint to whom the Great Hospital in Norwich was dedicated. It has been suggested that Giles may have been a saint to whom women felt a particular devotion (Binns 1989, 30). Indeed, his position as patron saint of beggars and cripples would have been consistent with the concern for charity shown especially by medieval women (Cullum 1992). St Paul was an appropriate patron for another hospital in the city of Norwich, because of his healing at the hands of Ananias (Acts 9:10-19). This episode, wherein Ananias restored Paul's sight, was followed by baptism, making him an especially appropriate model for the inmates of hospitals, who received both physical and spiritual care at these medieval institutions. The connection between physical and spiritual healing with baptism is further reflected in the popular choice of St John the Baptist as the patron saint of hospitals, including the foundation in Carbrooke.

The diocese's hospitals which were run for or by women maintained a number of sisters which varied and often changed over time. At St Giles, or the Great Hospital, in Norwich, for example, the initial foundation included four sisters; in 1420, however, only two were recorded (Knowles and Hadcock 1971, 381). St Paul's, by contrast, supported at least fourteen sisters throughout the period (Knowles and Hadcock 1971, 381). In addition to sisters, hospital staff included maid servants, as well as a warden or cleric who said masses, heard confessions, and administered the last rites. At the time of the suppression of St Paul's a female custodian, Agnes Lyon, had authority over staff and property of the hospital which was used 'for the comfort, relieff and lodgynges of pore straungers, vagrantes, syck and impotent persons' (NRO, DCN 48/26A/1).

Hospital sisters and brothers took vows and wore religious dress similar to those worn by cloistered nuns and monks. Most of the diocese's hospitals for women, in fact, followed the Rule of St Augustine, known as it was for its flexibility and emphasis on communal living, rather than on strict obedience to a superior. The flexibility of the Rule and of these institutions can be seen in the evolution during the eleventh and twelfth centuries of several small hospitals into female convents which continued to follow Augustine's ideals for communal life (Elkins 1988; Thompson 1991).

Female staff members were either 'whole' or 'half' sisters, implying a degree of regulation among their ranks. Most likely, the 'whole' sisters lived inside the hospital precincts, while 'half' sisters worked shifts in the hospital, but lived in their own homes. The institutes of St Paul's in Norwich, for example, specified that seven sisters reside within the hospital precincts, and seven live outside the hospital walls (Knowles and Hadcock 1971, 381). Like their cloistered counterparts, hospital sisters followed a daily routine of prayer; their day was, however, punctuated by tending to the poor and sick in their care. Nursing duties included bathing and feeding hospital inmates,

Hospitals, Informal Communities, and Individual Ascetics

as well as treating some ailments with herbal and medicinal remedies (Cullum 1991, 15). Hospital sisters were frequent recipients of testamentary bequests since their ministry to the sick and poor was considered spiritually as well as socially significant.

Further research will undoubtedly provide us with more information about the religious women who served medieval society's indigent. In the meantime, it is important to recognise the option that hospitals offered to medieval women who sought a communal religious lifestyle outside the more formal monastic cloister. Other women in the diocese who desired a religious life in community with others formed their own groups, thus creating another avenue for female piety. At least nine different groups of women lived together in the town of Ipswich, and in five different parishes in the city of Norwich, in the fifteenth and sixteenth centuries (Table 3). These informal groups were apparently not recognised by the institutional Church, nevertheless they were supported by local clerical and lay society. The precise identity, numbers, and details of these women's lives are unknown. What is certain is that their status was perceived as religious.

Our primary evidence for these small female communities comes from wills, where they appear as recipients of testamentary bequests. Will-makers referred to these women variously as, 'the women dedicated to chastity,' as 'sisters under religious vow,' as *'mulieres paupercule'* (poor women), and simply as *'sorores commeranti,'* or sisters living or staying together (PRO, PCC Prob 11/4/23; Blomefield 1805-10 vol. 4, 333; NRO, NCC 160 Brosyard; NRO, NCC 107 Wylbey). These descriptions do not necessarily denote religious status, although the emphasis on chastity, poverty, and a religious vow clearly signals some type of religious life. More concrete evidence for the religious nature of these communities is testators' perceptions of them. Their bequests to these groups of women are listed among those to the other religious persons and institutions remembered by the testators in their wills.

Some of these fifteenth-century groups have been noticed by previous historians. Blomefield, for example, noted the existence of the 'sisters under religious vow in the north-west corner of the churchyard' of St Peter Hungate; Tanner and Taylor mentioned the 'three sisters devoted to chastity' in the parish of St Lawrence (Blomefield 1805-10 vol. 4, 333; Tanner 1984, 203; Taylor 1821, 65). Other groups listed in Table 3, however, escaped the sights of these historians. Five groups of nuns, for example, continued to live together in small communities in Norwich city parishes after their monasteries had been dissolved. At least nine of the seventeen ex-prioresses and nuns who can be traced, including ex-nuns from Bruisyard, Bungay, Campsey Ash, and Shouldham, lived in the parish of St Stephen. Three of the ex-nuns of Carrow settled in Norwich in the parish of St Peter Hungate.

Further discoveries may yet be made about these improvised groups. The mystery of their origins and activities renders them difficult to define. The community in Westwyk, outside the Norwich city walls, for example, is described by Dunn as an anchorage, and by Knowles and Hadcock as a hospital (Dunn 1973, 27; Knowles and Hadcock 1971, 407). Yet the community is described in the fifteenth-century will of John Rich, priest of the church of St Michael of Coslany in Norwich, simply as 'the sisters dwelling in Westwyk' (NRO, NCC 151 Hyrnyng). Such ambiguity characterised all of the provisional religious communities, and served both as an asset and as a liability. Their informality may have accounted for the patronage of local testators, but probably for their eventual disappearance as well.

It is possible that the fifteenth-century communities in Norwich resembled beguinages, the communities of women found most commonly in the Low Countries in the twelfth and thirteenth centuries, as Tanner has suggested (Tanner 1984, 65, 130-131). Cultural and religious ideas and trends could easily have travelled the trade routes between the Low Countries and East Anglian ports. It is also possible, however, that the informal groups in the parishes of Norwich resembled *maisons dieu*: flexible, often short-lived communities of poor women and men found in many medieval English towns. In York, for example, the small hospitals and *maisons dieu* came to be increasingly occupied by poor women (Cullum 1992, 199). Informal groups in other areas have been mentioned in passing as well, like 'the poor women and widows living in Lymstrete' (Warren 1985, 229). These communities suggest a possible indigenous tradition of female piety, which flourished outside the theological and spiritual practices ordained by the Church, the existence of which we are only beginning to realise. The danger in classifying these groups into categories of religious life, such as beguinages, is that it may disguise the true nature of these communities, and so limit our understanding of female piety in medieval England.

While the precise character of these communities eludes us, we can partially reconstruct the lives of the women who created them. The groups of ex-nuns probably continued to follow to some extent the daily round of prayers which defined their lives in the cloister. Elizabeth Throckmorton, the last abbess of Denny Abbey in Cambridgeshire, and two of her fellow nuns retreated to her family's manor in Coughton where they continued to lead lives of prayer (*VCH, Cambridge* vol. 2, 301-302). The description of the other informal groups of religious women in wills suggests a certain public visibility which may have included charitable works, like visiting the sick and helping the poor. Such acts perhaps combined with the exemplary lives of these women to warrant the goodwill of medieval society.

Most of the diocese's informal communities were in Norwich, suggesting that the city itself attracted women interested in pursuing this type of religious life. Consider, for example, that the post-Dissolution communities of nuns were located in two of the same parishes, St Peter Hungate and St Stephen, where settlements of informal groups of women had existed in the fifteenth century. A surviving medieval building in Elmhill, possibly dated to the fifteenth century, is a candidate for the site of one such informal community. The house is situated at the top of Elmhill (number 9), adjacent to the east end of the church of the Blackfriars on its west, and backing onto the churchyard of St Peter Hungate on its south. A door from the churchyard provided direct access to the house, which consisted of three self-contained floors reached by an external stair on the east side. This building would have served as ideal accommodation for the informal community suggested at the site, or the group of nuns which sought refuge in the parish after the Dissolution (Plate 11). The parish of St Swithin's, where another band of women occupied the tenement of John Pellet, was also the site of an almshouse for women in the sixteenth century. While cities traditionally drew the unemployed in the Middle Ages, especially women, the continued presence of informal groups of religious women in these particular parishes from the fifteenth through the sixteenth centuries, indicates that the city of Norwich may have been a centre for this kind of female spiritual activity, and hints, moreover, of a type of female piety hitherto unrecognised.

While the details of the lives of these religious women in the city of Norwich remain unknown, John Bale, a Carmelite priest, wrote of a fifteenth-century community of women who lived in the town of Ipswich. His account tells that they lived by an informal rule which dictated that they rise at midnight from September 14 until Easter, at dawn in the summer; refrain from eating meat; fast on bread and ale on Fridays and Saturdays;

wear hairshirts, and above all, say 'a prodigious number of prayers' (Zimmerman 1891-1900, 198). These women were probably associated with the Carmelite friars in the same town, although the nature of the connection is unknown.

The Carmelite friars were associated with other religious women in the diocese. Numerous female anchorholds were established in Carmelite friaries in Norwich, Lynn, and Ipswich, as well as in other parts of England throughout the Middle Ages, indicating a strong connection between this

Plate 11: Elmhill, Norwich: the medieval building to the left (*c*fifteenth-century) may have housed an informal community of religious women living adjacent to the churchyard of St Peter Hungate. Nearby was the anchoress's cell attached to the church of the Blackfriars (background), represented by blocked archways beneath the traceried window.

mendicant order and medieval women who sought more solitary religious lives (Clay 1914; Knowles and Hadcock 1971). Table 4 lists all of the anchoresses known to date in the diocese of Norwich, from the earliest, Aelfwen, who lived in Hulme, Norfolk, in the eleventh century, to Katherine Mann, who was an anchoress at the Blackfriars in the city of Norwich, until at least 1555. Her anchorhold was adjacent to the tenement in Elmhill thought to have housed the informal group of religious women in the northwest corner of the churchyard of St Peter Hungate (Plate 11). Together they suggest another enclave of Norwich favoured by religious women and their patrons.

We can identify at least seventy-three anchoresses who lived at forty-two different sites in the diocese, fourteen of which were not previously known. By contrast, sites of male recluses in the diocese numbered thirty-two (Clay 1914, 232-237, 248-249). Most of the female anchorholds were in the county of Norfolk.

The predominance in Norfolk of this individual style of religious vocation is curious, but one of several factors may explain this geographical pattern. First, it is possible that a source bias has excluded many female anchorholds in the county of Suffolk. A list of anchorholds maintained by Bury St Edmunds Abbey, for example, includes some forty sites in Suffolk, Cambridgeshire, and Norfolk (Gransden 1960, 464). The list does not specify, however, if the recluses who inhabited these sites were female or male. It is likely, therefore, that more female anchorholds existed in Suffolk than we have been able to recover.

The relative absence of anchoresses in Suffolk might also reflect the power of the abbey on the county's ecclesiastical affairs, an influence which may have been inhospitable to anchoresses. On the other hand, anchoresses, like the informal religious communities of women, tended to be an urban phenomenon, a fact which is well illustrated by the number of female anchorholds sited in the city of Norwich.

Many of the city's anchorholds show a long tradition of female recluses, reinforcing our earlier suggestion that the city particularly attracted religious women in the Middle Ages. The Blackfriars, for example, maintained female recluses from at least the late fifteenth through the sixteenth centuries (Table 4). Even more impressive is the continuity of recluses at St Edward, Conisford, and at St Julian, Conisford, where we have evidence of anchoresses from the thirteenth to the sixteenth centuries, and from the fourteenth through the sixteenth centuries respectively. Julian of Norwich is perhaps the most famous of the city's anchoresses, but clearly she was not the only one whom the city supported.

Among the many other anchoresses who graced the city was Katherine Mann, a recluse at the Blackfriars, whose tenure there dated from at least 1531. Mann is perhaps best remembered for her association with Thomas Bilney who was burned at the stake in 1531 (Tanner 1984, 64, 163-164). She was highly literate, and her reputation as a holy and wise woman spread as far as London, from whence notable male clerics trekked seeking her counsel. Her local renown secured her anchorhold after the friar's house was suppressed in 1539. In 1548, the mayor of Norwich confirmed this grant and extended it for the rest of her life, and contributed additionally an annual pension of 20*s*. for her support. Two years later, the town conferred on her the privilege 'freely to occupy the city' (Dunn 1973, 22, 25).

Details about several other female recluses in the diocese reveal that they were women of various circumstances and levels of society. Margaret, a thirteenth-century anchoress at St Edward, Conisford, supported herself. Using her own seal, she conceded a tenement in Buthorp to the abbot of Langley in exchange for 6*s*. a year (Dunn 1973, 21). Sabine, a recluse enclosed at the church of St Saviour in Norwich, received 3*s*. annually from Albin of Stanford, as per the quitclaim of her mother, Matilda, widow of Alan of Thorp (Dodwell 1974-76 vol. 2, 40). Most of the other anchoresses are known only by their first names, suggesting that they were of lesser social standing than Margaret or Sabine, and so were dependent on the largess of their local communities and passers-by who benefited from the anchoresses' prayers.

Information on the standards of living maintained by anchoresses remains unclear, since anchorholds have not been subject to modern archaeological excavation. Surviving buildings and documentary evidence, however, indicate that the majority of anchoress's cells were located on the north side of the church with a squint allowing the anchoress to view the high altar. The anchorhold at St Edward, Conisford, for example, was sited on the north side of the church; so was the anchorhold at the Blackfriars (Blomefield 1805-10 vol. 4, 69-70, 72; Dunn 1973, 19). Evidence of the cell at the Blackfriars survives in the eastern end of the north wall of the friar's chancel, where three blocked brick archways suggest a single-story cell of more than one room abutting the church. Elsewhere structures to the north of the chancel may have been built as anchoresses' cells but were later converted for use as vestries. At St Andrew's church, Saxthorpe (Norfolk), a splayed squint (66.5 x 29 cm) communicated between the high altar and the cell, which has been substantially rebuilt. That it was used as a cell by the 'venerable Cecily' up to 1534 is suggested by a brass located to the west of the rood screen: *Hac jacent in tumba Cysly venerabilis Ossa, VIII die Maii AD MCCCCCXXXIIII. Orate, Orate.* The anchorhold of Julian of Norwich, at the church of St Julian, Conisford, has been reconstructed on the south side at the junction between the nave and the chancel, but there is no evidence to indicate its original medieval position or form. The north orientation of many female anchorholds is consistent with the north/female spiritual association identified earlier in this study, which was common in both early Christianity and also in other religious traditions.

Some anchorholds were simply a single cell, such as Leatherhead (Surrey), but others were more substantial two-story buildings, like the extant structure at Chester-le-Street (Durham), perhaps with an accommodation for a servant. It is possible that larger anchorholds were originally constructed to accommodate more than one anchoress. While recluses were supposed to live alone, there are several examples of anchoresses who lived in pairs. Ela and her companions, for example, were at Massingham in Norfolk, from at least 1256 to 1291, when they appear in the will of Bishop Walter of Suffield (Dunn 1973, 24). Margaret and Alice were enclosed together in a cell at the church of St Olave in 1298 (Clay 1914, 150). And Agnes and Helewise were both recluses at St Vedast in Norfolk (BL, Add. Ms 43,407 fol. 134v). Pairs of recluses like these are found only in the thirteenth century, suggesting that this practice ceased in the later Middle Ages.

Another early example of a group of female recluses is that of Leva of Lynn who, with her followers, sought out a solitary place to live in the manner of the Desert Fathers. Soon after Leva and her company settled in the fenland parish of Wiggenhall St Mary Magdalen, flooding forced them to move to another site; their second settlement was soon converted into the Augustinian priory of Crabhouse. What is interesting about Leva's original site is that one of her followers, Joanna, remained behind (Bateson 1892, 3-4, 13). The nuns at Crabhouse received the advowson of this hermitage where anchoresses continued to live (Blomefield 1805-10 vol. 9, 173). In 1492, Margaret Oldham left 12*d.* to 'every nun in the houses of the towns of Thetford, Shouldham, Wiggenhall, Blackborough, Cambridge, Chatteris, Swaffam, Denny, Iklyngton, Crabhouse, Bruisyard, Campsey Ash and Flixton,' indicating the presence of an anchoress in Wiggenhall as late as the fifteenth century (Tymms 1850, 73). In addition to this anchorhold, however, Crabhouse Priory maintained female recluses within the convent's walls in the thirteenth and fifteenth centuries (Table 4). Historians have quibbled over Leva and the origins of her foundations in Wiggenhall St Mary Magdalen, never acknowledging the presence of anchoresses at both sites throughout the Middle Ages (Thompson 1991, 24-25; *VCH, Suffolk* vol. 2, 408).

The presence of a female convent and a female anchorhold seems to have raised the profile of religious women in the Wiggenhall parishes. Next to the parish of Wiggenhall St Mary Magdalen, and on the same side of the River Ouse, was the parish of St Mary the Virgin, the advowson of which was held by the canons of Westacre Priory (Blomefield 1805-10 vol. 9, 181). The parish church of St Mary the Virgin retains benches with elaborately carved ends dated to the fifteenth century. Prominent among the figures carved on bench-ends in the southern half of the church are female saints and nuns. The rood screen in this church, dating also from the late medieval period, portrays eight saints. From north to south they are: St Mary Magdalen, holding an ointment box; St Dorothy, with a basket of flowers and fruit; St Margaret, plunging her cross into a dragon; St Scholastica, wearing a black cowl and a red cloak; St Catherine, wielding a sword; St Barbara, depicted with the tower in which her father held her prisoner; St Mary the Virgin with the Holy Child; and finally, St John the Baptist with the *Agnus Dei* (Aston 1990, 274). The predominance of female saints and figures in a medieval parish church is noteworthy, perhaps indicating that patrons wished to identify with the nearby female monastery and anchorholds.

Both female and male recluses were highly valued in medieval society for the prayers they sang daily for the souls of the living and the dead. Yet anchoresses' prayers were especially prized by medieval society. According to Church teachings, a woman's carnal nature made it more difficult for her to lead a spiritual life than it was for a man, especially if she chose the severe path of a recluse. While anchoresses did not necessarily internalise such views, the perceived inherent moral and physical inferiority of women added significance to their successful asceticism, and hence value to the prayers they said for the salvation of all souls. That more women than men pursued this life suggests that this vocation was particularly appealing to women, perhaps offering some degree of spiritual independence.

Another option available to women who desired to lead a private religious life was to become a vowess (Table 5). As described in Chapter 1, vowesses were widows who were veiled and given a ring in a ceremony presided over by a bishop, during which they vowed to lead chaste lives dedicated to prayer. Unlike anchoresses or other female recluses, however, vowesses were less strictly bound by the Church. They could live in their own home, like Margery Baxster in Heveningham, Suffolk; or they could reside within

Hospitals, Informal Communities, and Individual Ascetics

a religious community, as did many of the vowesses in the diocese of Norwich. Like nuns and anchoresses, vowesses were part of a long tradition of female religious life.

Records from the diocese of Lincoln include the vows which widows took, and certain biblical references to this religious state (Clarke 1971, 19-21). In early Christianity, widows who renounced further marriages were supported by alms donated by the Church. Later Church fathers, Ambrose and Augustine, instructed vowesses to perform pastoral duties, like tending the sick and acting as deaconesses in local churches. These theologians further advised the widows to pray continually for the souls of Christendom. Several medieval texts comprised similar advice to vowesses, and also counselled them to pray especially to St Anne, the patron saint of widows (Raymo 1986, 2320). Vowesses were especially commended for their chaste state, the most highly prized status for any woman in the medieval Church.

The position of an anchoress or vowess represented vocations for women who chose solitary religious lives. The last category of religious lifestyle in the diocese of Norwich includes women who were similarly alone in their vocations, as well as small groups of women who are referred to as nuns (Table 6). Wills provide the only evidence for these women, who were clearly seen by the testators as having religious status. Bequests to all of the women listed in Table 6 come among those to priests, nuns, parish churches and chapels, and other religious beneficiaries.

The nuns at West Dereham, a house of Premonstratensian canons, appear in the will of Baldwin Dereham of Crimplesham, dated 1527 (NRO, NCC 154-55 Hayward). While there is no evidence in any of Dereham Priory's extant records that the house maintained a cell of nuns, some Premonstratensian monasteries were originally double houses for women and men, including Broadholme (Nottinghamshire). At Domesday, certain Benedictine houses were listed as supporting cells of nuns, among them Bury St Edmunds, Ely, St Albans and Evesham. Perhaps the canons at Dereham accommodated a group of nuns who were not recorded in any Church documents. The nuns named in other places in Norfolk were similarly not referred to in any of the diocesan, episcopal, or other ecclesiastical records. While it might be suggested that these groups constituted almshouses or hospitals, the testators distinguished between the *sorores*, usually hospital sisters, and the *moniales*, or nuns, who received bequests. The women in Grenecroft, Hengham (?Hingham) and Swaffham were called *moniales*.

Similar small groups of nuns appeared in other parts of England in the twelfth and thirteenth centuries, which were often later regularised into convents or hospitals (Elkins 1988). The nuns in Norfolk are intriguing, especially at Dereham and Hengham, due to the late date of their appearance: 1527 and 1385 respectively. It is impossible to know whether these women considered their lives in community to be the same as the lives of cloistered nuns, and so called themselves nuns, or if local testators recognised them as such. Nevertheless, these women constituted part of the religious landscape of medieval Norfolk.

The individual religious women listed in Table 6 all appear in wills as 'mother'. It is possible that Mother Grene, a legatee in the 1551 will of William Elys, was Joanna Grene, who was a nun at Carrow in 1514. (NRO, NCC 196 Coraunt; Jessopp 1888, 145). Her disappearance from later visitation records makes this questionable, although if she was the same woman, she could have retained some sort of religious status after her departure from the convent. Perhaps these women were almswomen, midwives, or godmothers who were known and admired by the testators. While the identities of these women remain a mystery, it is important to note their religious status, at least as it was perceived by their contemporaries, and to acknowledge that this was yet another way in which women led religious lives in the diocese of Norwich.

Conclusion

This survey of religious women in the diocese of Norwich has revealed the range of options available to women and the significant contributions that they made to the spiritual culture of medieval Norfolk and Suffolk. Indeed, their presence received more attention and commanded greater respect from contemporary medieval society than has been realised previously.

Certain aspects of these women's lives displayed characteristics which were gender-related and specific to female piety. Nunneries, for example, were more akin in their construction to manorial gentry settlement than mainstream monasteries for men, particularly in the use of moats, courtyards, and privy facilities. Consider also that in contrast to their male counterparts, monasteries for women were never intended to be self-sufficient. Rather, the small initial endowments of marginal land made by founders may well have reflected the poverty and physical separation from society which nuns actively sought as a part of their religious vocations.

Poverty and physical separation from society were also characteristics of other holy women in the diocese, the hospital sisters, anchoresses, hermits, and the women who formed their own religious communities. Instead of being identified as negative attributes of female religious life, these choices should be considered in the wider context of female piety in the Middle Ages. Poverty and physical separation can be seen as part of the denigration of the body, a characteristic of female spirituality in the Middle Ages. Monastic seals which show Christ on the Cross, like those of Bungay and Flixton, reflected medieval women's devotion to Christ's Passion and Crucifixion thereby giving more material expression to this aspect of female piety.

Also gender-related seems to have been the greater involvement that the nuns maintained with their local communities. As more consistent alms-givers, for example, the nuns share in the tradition of women as nurturers and care-takers. Certainly the hospital sisters as well as the women who lived in less formal religious communities, and the 'mothers' who received

Conclusion

testamentary bequests, participated in providing physical and also spiritual sustenance and charity to those with whom they came in contact. This association of women as dispensers of charity was further reflected in the choice of St Giles and St Paul, figures of charity and healing, as patron saints of some of the diocese's hospitals for women.

Several aspects of the various female religious lifestyles suggest specific symbolic associations between women and female saints. The saints' dedications of some of the diocese's convents, to St Barbara and St Catherine in particular, show an abiding affiliation between women and female saints. Such an association between symbols and holy women was further reflected in the adoption of the north-sided cloister, as well as in the north-sided anchoress's cells in the diocese, a connection which reflected an earlier Christian tradition in which female saints were associated with the north sides of churches.

The ambiguity and flexibility which characterised the informal communities of women relates to broader issues which affected both religious and lay women in the Middle Ages. These communities can be seen as a response to the misogyny of the medieval Church and the ambivalence toward women that many Church Fathers expressed. As such, the enigma of the informal communities of women and certain unconventionalities of the more traditional options were necessary components of these religious women's vocations.

Women did not choose these paths as an escape from secular life, but rather because they had genuine religious vocations. The success of their lives and their value to society was well reflected in the consistent patronage which all of the religious women in the diocese attracted. The greater patronage that local gentry and yeoman farmers showed the nuns as compared to the diocese's monks and canons, for example, reflected both the social composition of the female monasteries and also the greater interaction which the nuns shared with their local communities. The strong tradition of female piety that existed in the medieval diocese of Norwich accords with its reputation as a region noted for a dynamic religious culture: a culture in which a landscape of female piety was essential.

Archaeological Gazetteer of East Anglian Nunneries

Norfolk

BLACKBOROUGH
NGR: TF 673 141
Founded in low, fenny ground on the River Nar, with reclamation to marshland. A sketch attached to the fifteenth-century cartulary gives a diagrammatic representation of lands acquired by the priory in the fourteenth century (BL MS Egerton 3137). The drawing depicts parcels of land owned by named individuals in relation to a rectory which has been identified as North Clenchwarton, on the basis of a name which occurs on the map and in charters of 1370 associated with Clenchwarton (Owen 1986).

On the site of the priory a section of wall survives running east-west, constructed of carstone with numerous putlog holes remaining. Further south is the gable-end and fragmentary walls of a more substantially built structure which formed the southern end of a north-south range. The gable has a small lancet window and ashlar buttresses. At the base of the eastern wall are two, two-centred brick arches, presumably for a drain to run through the southern part of the building. From this feature it may be suggested that the building functioned in part as a kitchen or latrine. If this building formed part of the main cloister the remains may represent the southern gable of the west or east ranges respectively. Alternatively both remaining buildings may have served as ancillary structures in an inner or outer court.

Nineteenth-century finds were reported including a number of stone coffins and two wooden coffins, one from a vault; corbels; and a number of small metal artefacts including a bronze strap-end with the inscription *IE XCE*. In the 1960s a tiled floor was uncovered of alternating black and yellow tiles, in addition to decorated tiles, twelfth-century and later glazed pottery, medieval glass and lead, and loose masonry including pillar bases and capitals.

CARROW
NGR: TG 242 074
The priory was built on marshy ground to the south of the town walls of Norwich.

Extensive remains include parts of the aisled cruciform Norman church, which survives east from the crossing, the south transept, and east and west ranges (Figure 5). The church terminates in a square-ended chancel, with bases of shafted Norman buttresses, transepts with chapels off, and an aisled nave. According to nineteenth-century excavations and the alignment of the chancel and nave, construction began from the east of the church in the mid-twelfth century, and the nave was completed in the early thirteenth. The entire interior of the church was lined with blank arcading, which survives in parts. The south wall of the south aisle and arcade cut earlier work, and may be of fifteenth to sixteenth-century date. On the north side of the chancel was the chapel to St Catherine; to the south are foundations of the chapel dedicated to St John the Baptist. A further chapel to the south of St John's was constructed over a plinth which runs continuously around the exterior of the east end, suggesting that this second chapel was a later addition. The sacristy projected east from the transept, and was entered from the transept through a doorway with refined mouldings and slender shafts.

Beyond the south transept was a slype containing remains of a circular stairway which gave access to the east range over the chapter-house; these stairs are likely to have served as the night-stairs of the nuns, giving direct access from the dormitory to the slype adjacent to the south transept. The chapter-house projected beyond the limit of the east range breaking forward beyond the outer line of the cloister. The day-stairs of the nuns were located to the south of the chapter-house, where a portion of dormitory wall retains the doorway which led from the day-stairs to the cloister. In the north-eastern corner of the cloister is a triangular-headed lamp locker. Domestic conversion of this range after the Dissolution included the placing of a fireplace in the chapter-house door. To the south of the chapter-house, the east range is represented by its west wall (extant in parts to upper storey level) and round pier bases. The dormitory was located at the upper level, and extended to the south beyond the limit of the rectangular cloister. At the south-west corner of the east range, an angled buttress joined the south range. Two vertical offsets formed of stone quoins are visible in the west face of the west wall, indicating the point at which the south and east ranges joined.

Attached to the east range, immediately south of the chapter-house, are the foundations of a small structure which are generally thought to represent the *reredorter*, or latrine block. The L-shape plan is indeed consistent with latrines excavated at nunneries elsewhere, however, its position at the northern end of the east range is most unusual. Latrines were generally positioned towards the southern end of the dormitory, at a greater distance from the church and chapter-house. Fragments of masonry to the east of the cloister, at the edge of the River Wensum, may represent the infirmary.

The west range was rebuilt by the prioress Isabel Wygun in the sixteenth century, and is wholly extant albeit heavily restored between 1899-1909 (Plate 5). The original medieval range is contained in the north half of the building from the present porch. It was constructed in a chequerwork of brick and flint nodules, galletted with broken flints. The priory guest house and prioress's lodge consisted of a hall, north parlour, and spiral staircase to an upper chamber with oriel window.

Extant features include moulded beams, doors and the parlour fireplace with its visual pun on the name of prioress Wygun (Y plus gun).

Resistivity survey confirmed that the cloister had been re-ordered, with the demolition of the original west range in order to build the prioress's lodge (Atkin and Gater 1983 unpub). The original line of the west range can be detected at the south-east corner of the cloister. The south range is largely intact below ground surface; a group of ancillary buildings further to the south may be suggested by anomolies shown by the resistivity survey. A possible infirmary cloister was suggested against the east wall of the dormitory.

Excavated areas include a cess pit outside the precinct located at the eastern entry, and the excavation of twelve burials from the church and its graveyard to the north (*Medieval Archaeol* 26 1982, 196). Interior burials were ranged mainly along the arcades of the choir; an additional three graves were placed in front of the chancel steps. One of the graves before the chancel steps was recognised as the burial of a priest on the basis of the chalice and paten by which it was accompanied (Atkin and Margeson 1983). With the exception of the priest, and a child buried in the graveyard, the skeletons were those of adult women. Excavations in the nineteenth century revealed burials to the east of the chapter-house, and a stone coffin to the south of the chancel. Occasional finds include an intact thirteenth-century cooking pot.

The church is unusually large for a female house. In fact, Carrow was larger than any other parish or monastic church in Norwich with the exception of the Cathedral Priory, although there is no evidence for access up to a gallery or triforium. The length of the church is directly comparable to the Cluniac church at Castle Acre, both 61m. The church, the chapter-house projecting from the range and the dormitory extended beyond the cloister indicate a house of unique status within the women's communities of medieval East Anglia.

CRABHOUSE
NGR: TF 601 078

Founded in fenland, later reclaimed to marshland given to frequent flooding, in the south of the parish of Wiggenhall St Mary Magdalen. Crabbe Abbey house now occupies the site; the house and garden contain many fragments of medieval masonry. Associated finds include pottery, metalwork, carved stone and human remains recorded in the eighteenth and nineteenth centuries (Norfolk SMR).

It is possible to partially reconstruct the layout of the priory on the basis of a survey conducted in 1557 (Dashwood 1859), which describes the dimensions of the buildings and courts which remained at that date (Figure 3). The precinct contained two large courts or yards to the west and north of the original cloister, of one acres and three roods (0.75 acre) respectively. At the time of the survey, entry to the courtyard was from a gate to the east, through a passage with walls eight foot in height. The west range and cloister of the original priory were retained after the Dissolution. The range was ordered as a hall with upper and lower ends. The chamber with solar at the upper end corresponds with details given for the construction of the prioress's lodgings in the Register of Crabhouse for 1422: 'Also in the same yere sche [the prioresse] made the sowthe eende of her chawmbur, fro the cloyster doore to the freytoure eende, there nevyr noon was beforne. And the tresense [entrance?] fro the chawmbur door to the halle doore, the which chawmbur and tresence cost XL marc.' (Bateson 1892, 57-8). This passage describes the construction of the chamber from the south end (the cloister door) to the north end (freytoure end) and the entrance between the hall and chamber. The survey and register imply that the refectory (freytoure) was sited as the north range of the cloister.

The survey describes the outbuildings in 1557, many of which seem to have dated to the occupation of the priory, such as the old mill house and old little storehouse. The parson's lodgings are described, consisting of chamber, buttery and kitchen, adjoining the old steeple. The nunnery church had been demolished by 1557, but the steeple and churchyard to the south-east are noted. Their situation confirms that the church formed the south range of the cloister. Entrance to the nave, which also served as a parish church, must have been from the south-west. The construction of the buildings was not elaborated in the survey. However, roofing materials were recorded, varying from slate (hall range, malting house) and tile (cattle pen) to reed (stables, storehouse, parson's lodgings, including kitchen with brick chimney).

MARHAM
NGR: TF 707 098

Founded on the edge of fen or marsh to the north-east and the river Nar to the north. The abbey was sited to the west of the parish church of Holy Trinity.

The south wall of the nave survives (Plate 7), constructed of limestone ashlar with remaining putlog holes and two large circular windows at clerestorey level (one quatrefoil, one sexfoil). Blomefield noted that four such windows were in existence in the eighteenth century; these may have been transferred to the tower of the parish church. Remains of internal wall-plaster survive at the east end of the section of wall. The cloister was formed by a walkway with pentice roof projecting from the south wall of the church, evidenced by the plinth and extant corbels which would have supported the lean-to roof.

The north end of the west range is partially extant, constructed of flint with brick quoins. This survival may represent a part of the guest house. It is separated from the remainder of the range by a partition wall of ashlar limestone, and consists of a fourteenth-century room which is rib-vaulted in two bays. In the south-east corner the ribs are supported by a half-figure of a bearded man who seems to be a knight holding a gauntlet or sword-hilt (Figure 4). Nichols has reconstructed a possible plan of the cloister which includes a cruciform church, cloister to the south, chapter-house projecting beyond the east range, and refectory projecting from the south range and aligned north-south in the Cistercian fashion. His reconstruction is entirely conjectural (Nichols 1978).

Aerial photographs reveal a number of complexes of earthworks within the precinct (Plate 2). To the south of the church the ranges flanking the cloister can be discerned. To the west is a ditched enclosure, with a rectangular outbuilding further west. A complex to the north-west of the cloister appears to be an infirmary with three ranges grouped around a courtyard. A number of depressions to the south may be fishponds.

SHOULDHAM
NGR: TF 680 095

The precinct was bounded by a wide ditch which survives in its north-west and north-east sections. A complex of fishponds is indicated to the north of the site.

The remains consist of earthworks to the south of Abbey Farm, including a moated enclosure (91.4m x 33.5m). Aerial photography has revealed crop marks to the north-east of the farm which represent the marks of the robber-trenches of the foundations of the monastic buildings (Edwards 1989) (Plate 9). These marks indicate the north transept and east end of the conventual church, with its three chapels. To the north of the chapels are foundation trenches of buildings which may include those of the chapter-house, and *reredorter* (latrine block), served by a drainage channel linked to a series of ditches south and south-east of the fishponds. These foundations suggest that the monastic cloister was located to the north of the main conventual church. On analogy with other Gilbertine double houses, this is likely to represent the cloister of the nuns. At Watton (Humberside) the nuns' cloister was positioned to the north of the main conventual church, with the canons' cloister and chapel situated some distance to the east.

Excavations in 1983 revealed complex stratigraphy and clunch-built walling which may represent the west range of the nuns' cloister (Rogerson 1983 unpub). Associated finds include a bronze lifting-tool for book pages or gold leaf.

THETFORD
NGR: TL 873 823

The nuns were transferred from Lyng, where associated finds include medieval pottery, a late Saxon pin and sceatta (Norfolk SMR). Founded first as a cell for monks of Bury St Edmunds, the priory was established on marshy ground. Its precinct was defined by the town walls to the north-west and the river to the south-east. There are indications of a fishpond to the east.

The medieval and later buildings exhibit an unusual quantity of fine ashlar limestone. This may relate to the situation of the priory near the ford of the rivers Thet and Little Ouse. Before the silting of the rivers sometime after the eleventh century, building stone would have been easily transported from northern France. The abundance of limestone may relate to the earlier occupation of the site by Bury St Edmunds while river transport was still possible.

Extensive remains of the twelfth century and later indicate an aisleless church with south transept, with portions of the chapter-house surviving to the south of the transept (Plate 8). The transept is entered through a wide two-centred arch from the crossing; the arch is of two orders on single half columns with Norman respond scallop capitals. East of the transept arch is a pilaster buttress; a second pilaster is further east. In the south-east corner of the transept there is a staircase to the upper storey of the east range which would have served as the night-stairs for the nuns. A partial plinth remains at the upper storey of the transept which most likely related to the post-Dissolution conversion of the church to domestic accommodation. At the east end of the south wall there is a blocked two-centred doorway which would have given access to the ground-floor of the east range. There are joist holes in the east wall at the south end and a window later blocked with a brick fireplace-stack and upper fireplace. The south wall of the church appears to be original twelfth-century fabric. Two blocked openings south of the transept suggest entrances to the church from the cloister alleys. In the south wall of the nave are three sixteenth-century three-light windows with hollow-chamfered mullions and rectangular hood-moulds on lozenge label stops. These appear to have been false windows related to the post-Dissolution domestic conversion of the church which involved the insertion of an upper floor to the nave and south transept; the windows in the south transept were originally open.

Much of the north wall seems to have been rebuilt in the fifteenth century, although evidence survives for an earlier arched opening to the north transept and a blocked archway possibly leading to a chapel. Fifteenth-century fabric includes two large windows in the north wall and one in the south transept east wall. In the north wall of the nave is an image niche at upper level.

To the south of the cloister, roughly in line with the east range, is a two-storey building in ashlar with a cell attached to the north end. The major structure consists of a two-storey hall (*c*fifteenth-century) which may have served as an infirmary with accommodation in an open dormitory at the upper level. The position of the hall in relation to the cloister supports the attribution of this function. Its north-south alignment, however, would have necessitated the positioning of an altar along the east wall, for which no evidence survives. The cell to the north, which has often been described as the infirmary chapel, was most likely a later addition with a separate function, such as guest accommodation. The stringcourse and coursing of the stone is not continuous between the hall and the structure to the north, which is a separate and self-contained structure with an external stair in the south-west corner. If this latter building had served as the infirmary chapel there would have been open access from the hall.

Recent excavations south of the transept indicated foundations for the *pulpitum* (screen) (Andrews forthcoming). The chapter-house was contained within the walls of the east range, its eastern limit defined by an extant wall. An early well was suggested in the area around the south range, the appropriate setting for a kitchen to serve the refectory.

Skeletons have been recorded around the exterior of the chancel and possibly to the west of the church; two early skeletons were excavated in the nave.

Suffolk

BRUISYARD
NGR: TM 334 662
Remains of the moated enclosure survive on three sides. Earthworks indicate fishponds to the north-west of the moat, and a long rectangular orchard enclosure, and remains of buildings within the grounds of the later house. Excavations in 1948 recorded finds of glazed or encaustic tiles (Suffolk SMR).

There is evidence for extant medieval fabric in the west wall and front of the south facade of the present early seventeenth-century house. That in the west wall incorporates flint rubble walling and two blocked two-centred arches. A room in the west range with a heavily beamed ceiling may have formed part of the medieval nunnery.

BUNGAY
NGR: TM 337 897
The broad aisled nave of the church survives as the principal parish church of Bungay, noted for its impressive south-west tower begun *c*1470. The church was originally cruciform, with the nunnery church as the eastern part. Fragments of precinct wall survive *in situ* in St Mary's Street, and Trinity Street. Remains of the priory church survive attached to the present chancel, although the ruins are on a slightly different orientation from the parish church. The claustral buildings were destroyed by fire in 1688.

Remaining fabric suggests that the nunnery cloister joined the church to the north, and an arched opening led to a chapel to the south. Remains of the priory include the walls of the north transept and parts of the nuns' choir. From the east, a doorway cuts through three windows of $c1300$. This may be repositioned or could represent an entrance to the sacristy. The nuns' choir retains a lancet and image niche and a stringcourse which runs for the length of the wall. The main door through the north wall is a two-centred arch with five moulded orders and ogee openings to either side. This door, and a second further south, both respect the stringcourse and appear to be *in situ*. The junction with the west range may be suggested at the point of a robbed buttress to the east of the transept, and by putlog holes in the east wall of the transept.

CAMPSEY ASH
NGR: TM 318 545

Founded on low ground near the River Deben. In 1347 the widow Maud de Ufford entered the house and a chantry college of five chaplains was endowed. They were to pray in the chapel of St Nicholas in the conventual church, and were provided with their own dormitory and refectory 'within the close near to the chapel' (Sherlock 1971, 121). Pevsner (1961) suggested that part of the college survives inside the present house (Ash Abbey), where there is evidence for a timber building with a fourteenth-century raised-aisle type roof. Extant medieval fabric includes a large barn, re-used stonework in other outbuildings and possibly the watermill which possesses a clasped purlin roof with an arched embattled tie-beam at the south-east end (Sherlock 1971, 123). The stream feeding the mill divides the precinct area, so that the cloister was situated to the east and the mill and outer court to the west. Remains of extensive fishponds survive. A plan of the ruins published in 1790 indicates an aisleless church forming the north range of the cloister, with an extant west range, a chapel of St Mary in the south range, and a dwelling house to the south of the cloister (in John Nichols' *Bibliotheca Topographic Britannica* 1790).

The present barn appears to have been the original west range of the priory. Its east wall has a small blocked thirteenth-century doorway at the north end. Stone moulding runs for most of the length of the building, indicating the line of a pentice roof for the west cloister walk (Plate 10).

Excavations on the site of the church in the 1960s revealed an area near the south aisle of the choir which contained burials of the priory's most important patrons, the Uffords. A private burial chapel was suggested by the situation of a pier base between the choir and aisle. Evidence was recovered for internal thresholds, six burials, Purbeck marble tombstones, a Purbeck marble tomb with brick partitioned chamber, and a leaden *bulla* of Pope Clement VI (1342 - 1352), buried with the Uffords in the easternmost area. The family was distinguished further by ceramic tiles which bear the Uffords arms and the initials BM (*Beata Maria*); the most common tile design is the cross engrailed with a crude fleur-de-lis and the initials

BM in two corners. An important group of tiles in relief design consists of animal designs moulded in high round-relief. Similar tiles have been recorded at the monastic houses of Castle Acre, Butley and Leiston (Keen 1971, 141). The church was constructed in flint with stone dressings of white Caen limestone, Lincolnshire limestone, greyish green sandstone, Septaria from the Thames basin and local materials including flint, Norfolk carstone and red crag. Twenty small fragments of window glass were recorded, some comparable to local grisaille of the mid-thirteenth century, and others coloured blue, green and maroon. Evidence for domestic occupation was recorded, including oyster shells, bones of small birds and animals (chicken, rabbit, etc).

FLIXTON
NGR: TM 315 863
Remains of the priory are situated approximately half a kilometre south-east of the ruined parish church, and consist of a single length of wall with an arch, within an irregular moated enclosure. The present Abbey Farm contains medieval fabric, including parts of two windows and rubble walling. The upstanding wall may have been part of the refectory or church; likewise the present farm may incorporate the church or refectory. The space between the two represents the area of the cloister, but it is not clear whether this stood to the north or south of the church. A survey of the site in *c*1581 noted that the demolished buildings had stood within the moat, and that outbuildings containing the guest accommodation survived until that time (Ridgard 1970).

REDLINGFIELD
NGR: TM 186 706
Part of a moat survives to the west of the site, possibly the original precinct boundary. The nuns shared the parish church of St Andrew, constructed in flint rubble. In its present state the church retains an aisleless medieval nave with a piscina at the east end of the south wall. The later chancel contains reset medieval features including a window with Y-tracery and doorway with two-centred arch. The nuns' church may have originally joined the nave to the east. Due to the position of the nunnery to the south, parochial access to the nave may have been restricted to a north door, now blocked, parallel with the south door and porch.

About 36 metres to the south of the parish church of St Andrew is a building of the medieval nunnery, now converted to a barn. This structure is aligned north-south, slightly to the west of a line projected from the south porch of the parish church (Plate 4). From the alignment of the building and its distance from the church it may be suggested that it was not part of the monastic cloister, which would be expected to have abutted the chancel of the parish church, but instead represents part of the inner or outer court.

The building measures approximately 16.4 x 4.5m and is constructed of flint rubble (with later rendering and brick patching), angled buttresses, and ashlar quoins and windows. The north wall retains two pointed arched openings at its base, possibly relating to a system of vaulting or to a conduit (Plate 3). Smaller arched openings in brick were observed during building conversion operations at St Olave's Priory (Suffolk) (E. Rose pers. com.) and at Blackborough (above); these appear to have related to a drain which would have flushed waste from the building, which may have functioned as a kitchen or ancillary domestic structure. Entrances in the west wall are indicated by two adjacent two-centred brick arches (with a modern entrance through the northern, and the southern blocked). At the south-western angle there are indications of the beginning of a wall projecting south from the range. The south elevation retains the remains of an ashlar doorway from its base to the springing point of the arch, and possibly the remains of a plinth at upper storey level. There are square-headed windows on the ground and first floor.

The substantial construction of the building suggests that it served as accommodation, perhaps as a detached guesthouse or residence for seculars known to have lived in the precinct; the inventory taken in 1536 mentions various chambers including that of the priory's servants and that of Master Donstone, possibly the chaplain (Hazlewood 1894).

Tables

Table 1. Monasteries for Women in the Diocese of Norwich

Name	Place[1]	Order[2]	Founder	Fnd	Dates Diss	Value in £s[3]
Blackborough	N	B	Muriel & Rbt de Scales	c1200	1537	42
Bruisyard	S	PC	Lionel, Duke of Clarence	1366	1539	56
Bungay	S	B	Gundreda & Rog Glanville	1160	1536	61
Campsey Ash	S	A	Agnes & Joan de Valoine	1195	1536	182
Carrow	N	B	King Stephen	c1146	1536	64
Crabhouse	N	A	Leva of Lynn	1181	1537	24
Flixton	S	A	Margery de Creyk	1258	1536	23
Marham	N	C	Isabel of Arundel	1249	1536	33
Redlingfield	S	B	Emma of Redlingfield	1120	1537	67
Shouldham	N	G	Geoffrey Fitz Piers	1148	1539	138
Thetford	N	B	Abbot Hugh of Bury St. Edmunds	c1160	1537	40

1. N = Norfolk; S = Suffolk.
2. B = Benedictine; PC = Poor Clares; A = Augustinian; C = Cistercian; G = Gilbertine
3. Values are rounded off to the nearest £; see: Caley and Hunter, *Valor Ecclesiasticus*.

Tables

St Stephen	Sisters living together there; ex-nuns of Bruisyard Abbey, Bungay, Campsey Ash, Carrow, and Shouldham Priories	1538-46	Baskerville, p. 211; NRO, NCC 19-20 Underwood: Elizabeth Loveday NRO, NCC 169 Puntyng:
	settled here post Dissolution		Thos Cappe NRO, NCC 261 Hyll: Ela Buttery
St Swithin	Sisters dedicated to chastity in a tenement of John Pellet; sisters dwelling there; almshouse for women	1427 1430-45 1570	Tanner, p. 203; NRO, NCC 30 Wylby: Thos Wetherby Taylor, p. 65
Norwich Suburb, Westwyk	Sisters dwelling	1417 1426	NRO, NCC 107 WylbyJohn Excester NRO, NCC 151 Hyrnyng: John Rich

1. **N** = Norfolk; **S** = Suffolk.

Tables

Table 4. Anchoress's Sites in the Diocese of Norwich

Place[1]	Name of Anchoress	Dates	Sources
Brandiston N	Margery de Boton	1526	Clay, pp. 232-33
Bury St Edmunds S	Dame Lucy	cKing John	Clay, p. 107
Clare S	Beatrice	1426	PRO, PCC PROB 11/3/6: Alice Howard
Cowlinge S	Nichola	1234	Clay, pp. 248-49
Coxford N	?	1537	Warren, p. 217
Fordham N	Isabel and Olive	?	Clay, p. 130
Framlingham S	?	1384	NRO, NCC 46 Harsyk: William Gerney, Kt
Heacham N	Sara	?	Warren, p. 157
Hulme N	Aelfwen	11th cent.	Clay, pp. 232-33
Hulme	Matilda Bylyngton	1286	Dodwell, 2:pp. 129-30
Husted (Horstead, N?)	Matilda	1268-75	BL, Add. Ms.43,407 fol. 144r
Ipswich S Carmelite Friary	Agnes	?	Clay, pp. 248-49
Lynn N Lynn	?	1504	NRO, ANW 60 Cook: Thos Herynyg
Carmelite Friars	Joanna Catefeld	1421	Clay, p. 78
East Gate	Anne Whyote	1384-86	Clay, p. 232
Friars' Minor	?	1483	NRO, DN/REG 17/12 fol. 245v
All Saints, South Lynn	Alice Belle	?	Hillen, p. 250
South Lynn	Isabella	1449	Clay, pp. 232-33
Martham N	Olive de Raveningham	13th cent.	Clay, pp. 232-33
Massingham N	Ela and	1256	Clay, p. 130 companions
Norwich N Black Friars	Katherine Foster	1481	Clay, pp. 234-35
Black Friars	?	1497/98	NRO, NCC 90 Multon: Katherine Kerre

Tables

Black Friars	Katherine Mann	1531-55	Tanner, pp. 163-64
Carmelite Friars	Emma de Stapildon	1422-42	Clay, pp. 77, 137
Carrow Priory	?	cKing John	Taylor, p. 65
Carrow Priory	Juliana	1443	Harrod, 4: pp.331-32
Carrow Priory	?	1446	Clay, p. 110
Carrow Priory	?	1497/98	NRO, NCC 90 Multon: Katherine Kerre
Carrow Priory	Margaret Kidman	-1546	Clay, pp. 234-35
St Bartholomew, Berstreet	Katherine	1306	Dunn, p.21
St Edward, Conisford	Margaret	13th c.	Clay, pp. 110-11
St Edward, Conisford	Margaret	13th c.	BL, Add. Ch. 14,558
St Edward, Conisford	Joan	1428	Clay, pp. 234-35
St Edward, Conisford	Agnes Kyte	1458	Ibid.
St Edward, Conisford	?	1516	Harrod, 1: p. 124
St George, Colegate	Margery	1291	NRO, DCN/70/2/1
St Giles	Katherine	1244	Blomefield, 4: p. 72
St James, Pokethorp	?	1422	Taylor, p. 65
St Julian, Conisford	Julian	1373-1413	Clay, pp. 234-35
St Julian, Conisford	Julian Lampit	1428-78	Ibid.
St Julian, Conisford	Julian Lampit	1463	Tymms, pp. 25-44
St Julian, Conisford	?Agnes	1472	NRO, NCC 30 Wylbey: Thos Wetherby
St Julian, Conisford	Elizabeth Scott	1481	Ibid.
St Julian, Conisford	?	1504	NRO, ANW 60 Cook: Thos Herynyg
St Julian, Conisford	?	1506	NRO, ANW 79 Cook: Robt Sevard
St Julian, Conisford	?	1510	NRO, ANW 88 Cook: Jone Chaunt
St Julian, Conisford	Elizabeth	1511	NRO, ANW 97 Cook: Thos Chaunt
St Julian, Conisford	?(to that other) Could she be at Carrow?	1511	Ibid.
St Julian, Conisford	Agnes Edrygge	1524	NRO, NCC 30 Wylbey: Thos Wetherby
St Julian, Conisford	?	1537/38	NRO, NCC 58-9 Underwood: Anne Esood
St Julian, Conisford	?	1547	Dunn, p. 25

Tables

St Margaret, Newbrigge	Katherine	1305, 1315	Clay, pp. 234-35 Dunn, p.19 Rye, p.103
St Mary, Coslany	St Anne's anchoress	?	Clay, pp. 234-35
St Michael, Coslany	?	1537	NRO, NCC 51-2 Hyll: Robt Corbeye
St Mary, Combuste	Cecily	1304-05	Clay, pp. 234-35 Dunn, p. 21 Rye, p. 100
St Michael at Plea	Agnes	1256-68	BL, Add. Ms. 43,407, fol. 134v
St Olave	Margaret and Alice	1289	Clay, p. 150
St Saviour	Sabine	13th c. 1304/05	Dodwell, 2: p. 40 Blomefield, 4: p.444
St Vedast	Agnes and Helewise	1256-68	BL, Add. Ms. 43,407 fol. 134v
? Saxthorpe N	'Venerable Cecily'	d.1534	funerary brass
Sudbury S			
St Gregory	2 sisters	13th c.	Warren, p. 33
	Matilda	1426	PRO, PCC PROB 11/3/6: Alice Howard
	Matilda	1431	PRO, PCC PROB 11/3/6: Walter Arnald
Walsingham N			
Walsingham	?	1497/98	NRO, NCC 90 Multon: Katherine Kerre
Walsingham	?	1504	NRO, NCC 60 Cook: Thos Herynyg
Walsingham	?	1530	NRO, NCC 76-8 Alpe: Richard Manser
West Winch N	Mabilia de Leverington	?	Clay, pp. 236-37
Wiggenhall N			
Wiggenhall	Johanna	+1180	Bateson, p. 3
Wiggenhall	Leva	-1180	Ibid.
Wiggenhall	?(nun)	1492	Tymms, p. 73
Crabhouse Priory	?	13th cent.	NRO, DCN 44/76/94
Crabhouse Priory	?	1417	NRO, NCC 27-8 Hyrnyng: Andrew Hooker

1. **N** = Norfolk; **S** = Suffolk.

Tables

Table 5. Vowesses in the Diocese of Norwich

Place[1]	Name	Dates	Sources
Blackborough Priory N	Joan Bumstede	1447	NRO, NCC 130-32 Wylbey: Joan Bardolf
	Alice de Branges	1457	NRO, NCC 58-9 Brosyerd: Kathryn Brasyer
	Dame Emma	1464	NRO, NCC 329-30 Brosyerd: Cathryn Goodrede
Campsey Ash Priory S	Isabel, Countess of Suffolk	1381	Suckling, 1: 171
Carrow Priory N	Dorothy Curson	1520	NRO, Hare 5455 227x1
Crabhouse Priory N	Margery	1497	NRO, NCC 90-1 Multon: Katherine Kerre
Flixton Priory N	Alice Brakenest of Halesworth	1381	BL, Stowe Ch. 348
Frenze N	Joan, widow of Sir John Braham	1519	Clayton, p. 131
Heveningham S	Margery Baxster aka Page	1533	SRO, ASF 12/169: Margery's will
Swaffham N	Jane Fraunk	1377	*Ely Diocesan Remembrancer*, May-June (1895), no.120
Thompson N	Joan, widow of Sir John de Shardelowe	1369	Blomefield, 2: 367
Witton N	Juliane Anyell	1500	Clayton, p. 131

1. **N** = Norfolk; **S** = Suffolk.
Note: For the vowesses at Campsey Ash, Frenze, Swaffham, Thornage, and Witton, we are indebted to Mary Erler, Dept of English, Fordham University, New York; and to Judith Middleton-Stewart for the vowess at Heveningham.

Tables

Table 6. Other Religious Women in the Diocese of Norwich

Place[1]	Description	Dates	Source
Dereham N	Nuns	1527	NRO, NCC 154-5 Hayward: Baldwin Dereham
Grenecroft N	Nuns	1280	NRO, BL vi (a) i
Hengham N (?Hingham)	Nuns	1385	NRO, NCC 58 Harsyk:John Polham
Norwich N	Mother there	1515	NRO, ANF 29 Batman: Clement Abbys
	Mother Love	1524	NRO, NCC 57-9 Grundisburgh:Agnes Abbastyre
	Mother Grene	1551	NRO, NCC 196 Coraunt: William Elys
Swaffham N	Nuns	1242, 1280	NRO, Norwich City Records 24 b (7); NRO, BL vi (a) i
Yarmouth N	Church for two nuns	1291	NRO, DCN 70/2/1
Unknown	Mother Turner Mother Taylor Mother Lawrence Mother Eyvse Mother Adams	1530	SRO, ASF, vii, 27: Margaret Ancell

1. **N** = Norfolk.

SRO, HD 1538/156/7
SRO, HD 1538/156/14
SRO, HD 1538/156/17
SRO, HD 1538/327
SRO, HD 1538/345

Unpublished Sources

Atkin, M. W. and J. A. Gater. *Carrow Priory, Norwich, Resistivity Survey.* Unpublished, 1983.

Nichols, J. 'The History and Cartulary of the Cistercian Nuns of Marham Abbey.' Ph.D. diss., Kent State University, 1974.

Oliva, M. 'The Convent and the Community in the Diocese of Norwich from 1350 to 1540.' Ph.D. diss., Fordham University, 1991.

Ridgard, J. M. 'The Social and Economic History of Flixton in South Elmham, Suffolk, 1300-1600.' M. A. Thesis, Leicester University, 1970.

Rogerson, A.J.G.R. 'Report of a Watching Brief at Shouldham Abbey, Norfolk', unpub. report in the Norfolk Archaeological Unit Sites and Monuments Record, 1983.

Published Sources:

Andrews, P. 'St. George's Nunnery, Thetford.' *NA*, forthcoming.

Aston, M. *Lollards and Reformers: Images and Literacy in Late Medieval Religion.* London, 1984.

Aston, M. 'Segregation in Church.' In *Women in the Church, Studies in Church History* 27, 237-294. Edited by W. J. Sheils and D. Wood. Oxford, 1990.

Atkin, M. W. and S. Margeson. 'A 14th-Century Pewter Chalice and Paten from Carrow Priory, Norwich.' *NA* 38 (1983): 374-379.

Baskerville, G. 'Married Clergy and Pensioned Religious in Norwich Diocese, 1555.' *EHR* 48 (1933): 43-46, 199-228.

Baskerville, G. *English Monks and the Suppression of the Monasteries.* New Haven, 1937.

Bateson, M., ed. 'The Register of Crabhouse Nunnery.' *NA* 11 (1892): 1-71.

Binns, A. *Dedications of Monastic Houses in England and Wales 1066-1216.* Woodbridge, 1989.

Bliss, W. H. and J. A. Twemlow, eds. *Calendar of Entries in the Papal Registers relating to Great Britain and Ireland: Papal Letters.* London, 1893-1819.

Blomefield, F. *An Essay toward a Topographical History of the County of Norfolk.* 11 vols. London, 1805-1810.

Brock, E.P.L. 'On the Excavation of the Site of Carrow Abbey, Norwich, by J. J. Colman, Esq. M. P., in 1880-1881.' *Journal of British Archaeological Association* 38 (1882): 165-214.

Bourdillon, A. *The Order of Minoresses in England.* Manchester, 1965.

Brown, P., ed. *Domesday Book Norfolk.* A Survey of the Counties of England Volume 33. General ed. J Morris. Chichester, 1984.

Burton, J. *The Yorkshire Nunneries in the Twelfth and Thirteenth Centuries.* York: Borthwick papers, no. 56, 1979.

Bynum, C. W. *Jesus as Mother: Studies in the Spirituality of the High Middle Ages.* Berkeley, 1982.

Bynum, C. W. *Holy Feast and Holy Fast: The Religious Significance of Food to Medieval Women.* Berkeley, 1987.

Calendar of Close Rolls. London: HMSO, 1906-1939.

Calendar of Patent Rolls. London: HMSO, 1905-1916.

Caley, J. and J. Hunter, eds. *Valor Ecclesiasticus.* 7 vols. London, 1810-1834.

Carr, R. D., A. Tester, and P. Murphy. 'The Middle Saxon Settlement at Staunch Meadow, Brandon.' *Antiquity* 62 (1988): 371-380.

Carthew, G. A. 'A Cellarer's Account Roll of Creake Abbey, 5 and 6 Edward III.' *NA* 6 (1864): 314-359.

Cheney, C. 'Norwich Cathedral Priory in the Fourteenth Century.' *Bulletin of the John Rylands Library* 20 (1936): 93-120.

Chettle, H. F. and E. Loftus. *A History of Barking Abbey.* Essex, 1954.

Clarke, A., ed. *Lincoln Diocese Documents 1440-1544.* Early English Text Society, o.s. 149, 1971 reprint.

Clay, R. M. *The Hermits and Anchorites of England.* London, 1914.

Clayton, M. *A Catalogue of Rubbings of Brasses and Incised Slabs. Victoria and Albert Museum.* London, 1929.

Coulton, G. G. 'The Truth about the Monasteries.' In *Ten Medieval Studies*, edited by G. G. Coulton, 3rd edtn, 84-107. Cambridge, 1930.

Cullum, P. H. *Cremetts and Corrodies: Care of the Poor and Sick at St. Leonard's Hospital, York in the Middle Ages.* York, 1991.

Cullum, P. H. "'And Hir Name was Charite': Charitable Giving by and for Women in late Medieval Yorkshire." In *Woman is a Worthy Wight. Women in English Society c.1200-1500*, edited by P.J.P. Goldberg, 182-211. Stroud, 1992.

Dashwood, G. H. 'Notes of Deeds and Survey of Crabhouse Nunnery, Norfolk.' *NA* 5 (1859): 257-262.

Denny, A. H., ed. *The Sibton Abbey Estates; Selected Documents, 1325-1509.* Suffolk Record Society Publications, vol. 2, 1960.

Devlin, D. 'Feminine Lay Piety in the High Middle Ages: The Beguines.' In *Medieval Religious Women*, vol. 1, *Distant Echoes*, edited by J. Nichols and L. Shank, 183-195. Kalamazoo, 1984.

Dodwell, B., ed. *The Charters of Norwich Cathedral Priory*, 2 vols. London, 1974-1976.

Dugdale, W. ed. *Monasticon Anglicanum.* 8 vols in 6. London, (1655-73) 1817-1840.

Dunn, F. I. 'Hermits, Anchorites and Recluses: A Study with Reference to Medieval Norwich.' In *Julian and Her Norwich: Commemorative Essays*, edited by F. D. Sayer, 18-26. Norwich, 1973.

Dymond, D. *The Norfolk Landscape.* Bury, 1990.

Edwards, D. A. 'Norfolk Churches, Air Photography and the Summer of 1989.' *Bulletin of the CBA Churches Committee* 26 (1989): 4-7.

Elkins, S. *Holy Women of Twelfth-Century England.* Chapel Hill, North Carolina, 1988.

Fernie, E. 'Carrow Priory, Norwich.' *Archaeological Journal* 137 (1979): 290-291.

Fleming, P. W. 'Charity, Faith, and the Gentry of Kent, 1422-1529.' In *Property and Politics*, edited by A. J. Pollard, 36-84. Stroud, 1984.

Foot, M. *Pictoral Bookbindings.* London, 1986.

Fosbrooke, T. *British Monachism, or Manners and Customs of the Monks and Nuns of England.* London, 1817.

Gairdner, J. 'A Letter Concerning Bishop Fisher and Thomas More.' *EHR* 7 (1892): 712-715.

Gasquet, F. A. *English Monastic Life.* London, 1905.

Gilchrist, R. "Blessed Art Thou Among Women': The Archaeology of Female Piety.' In *Woman Is A Worthy Wight. Women in English Society c.1200-1500*, edited by J.P.J. Goldberg, 212-226. Stroud, 1992.

Gilchrist, R. *Gender and Material Culture: The Archaeology of Religious Women.* London, 1993.

Gransden, A. 'The Reply of a Fourteenth-century Abbot of Bury St. Edmunds to a Man's Petition to be a Recluse.' *EHR* 75 (1960): 464-467.

Harrod, H. 'On the Mantle and the Ring of Widowhood.' *Archaeologia* 40 (1844): 307-310.

Harrod, H. 'Extracts from Early Wills in the Norfolk Registers.' *NA* 4 (1855): 317-339.

Harrod, H. 'Extracts from Early Norfolk Wills.' *NA* 1 (1874): 111-128.

Harrod, H. *Report on the Deeds and Records of the Borough of King's Lynn.* King's Lynn, 1874.

Hazlewood, F. 'Inventories of the Monasteries Suppressed in 1536.' *PSIA* 8 (1894): 83-116.

Heath, P. 'Urban Piety in the Later Middle Ages: The Evidence of Hull Wills.' In *The Church, Politics, and Patronage in the Fifteenth Century*, edited by B. Dobson. Stroud, 1984.

Hillen, H. *History of the Borough of King's Lynn*. 2 vols, Norwich, 1978.

Jacob, E. 'Two Documents Relating to Thomas Broun, Bishop of Norwich.' *NA* 33:4 (1965): 427-449.

Jessopp, A., ed. *Visitations of the Diocese of Norwich, 1492-1532*. London: Camden Society, n.s. 51, 1888.

Johnson, P. '*Mulier et Monialis*: The Medieval Nun's Self-Image.' *Thought* 64 (1989): 242-253.

Kearney, E. 'Heloise: Inquiry and the *Sacra Pagina*.' In *Ambiguous Realities: Women in the Middle Ages and Renaissance*, edited by C. Levin and J. Watson, 66-81. Detroit, 1987.

Keen, L. 'Medieval Floor-tiles from Campsea Ash Priory.' *PSIA* 32.2 (1971): 140-151.

Ker, N. R. *Medieval Libraries of Great Britain: A List of Surviving Books*. London, 1964.

Knowles, D. *The Monastic Order in England*. Cambridge, 1941.

Knowles, D. *The Religious Orders in England*, 3 vols. Cambridge, 1948, 1955, 1959.

Knowles, D. and R. N. Hadcock, eds. *Medieval Religious Houses in England and Wales*. London, 1971.

Leclercq, J. 'Hospitality and Monastic Prayer.' *Cistercian Studies* 8.1 (1973): 3-24.

Liveing, H.G.D. *The Records of Romsey Abbey*. Winchester, 1906.

Manning, C. R. 'A Monumental Brass Discovered under the Pews in St Stephen's Church, Norwich.' *NA* 6 (1864): 295-9.

Martin, T. *The History of the Town of Thetford, in the Counties of Norfolk and Suffolk, from the Earliest Account to the Present Time*. 1779.

McLaughlin, E. C. 'Equality of Souls, Inequality of Sexes: Women in Medieval Theology.' In *Religion and Sexism: Images of Woman in the Jewish and Christian Traditions*, edited by R. Ruether, 213-266. New York, 1974.

McNamara, J. A. 'Chaste Marriage and Clerical Celibacy.' In *Sexual Practices and the Medieval Church*, edited by V. Bullough and J. Brundage, 22-33. New York, 1982.

Messent, C.J.W. *The Monastic Remains of Norfolk and Suffolk*. Norwich, 1934.

Mortimer, R., ed. *Leiston Abbey Cartulary and Butley Priory Charters*. Woodbridge, 1979.

Nicholas, N., ed. *Testamenta Vetusta: Being Illustrations from Wills of Manners and Customs*. 2 vols. London, 1826.

Nichols, J. 'The Architectural and Physical Features of an English Cistercian Nunnery.' In *Cistercian Ideals and Reality*, edited by J. R. Sommerfeldt, 319-328. Kalamazoo, 1978.

Nichols, J. *Bibliotheca Topographica Britannica*. London, 1790.

Oliva, M. 'Aristocracy or Meritocracy? Office-holding Patterns in Late Medieval English Nunneries.' In *Women in the Church*, edited by W. J. Sheils and D. Wood, 197-208. Oxford, 1990.

Oliva, M. *The Convent and the Community in Late Medieval England*. Woodbridge, forthcoming, 1994.

Owen, D. M. 'Clenchwarton.' In *Local Maps and Plans from Medieval England*, edited by R. A. Skelton and P. D. A. Harvey, 128-30. Oxford, 1986.

Page, W., ed. *The Victoria History of the County of Norfolk*, vol. 2. London, 1906.

Page, W., ed. *The Victoria History of the County of Suffolk*, vol. 2. London, 1911.

Pevsner, N. *The Buildings of England: North-east Norfolk and Norwich*. Harmondsworth, 1962.

Pevsner, N. *The Buildings of England: North-west Norfolk and South Norfolk*. Harmondsworth, 1962.

Pevsner, N. *The Buildings of England: Suffolk*. Harmondsworth, 1961.

Phipson, M. R. 'Notes on Carrow Priory, Norwich.' *NA* 9 (1881): 215-225.

Power, E. *Medieval English Nunneries*. Cambridge, 1922.

Raven, J. J. 'The Ecclesiastical Remains of Bungay.' *PSIA* 4 (1874): 63-77.

Raymo, R. 'Works of Religious and Philosophical Instruction.' In *A Manual of the Writings in Middle English*, edited by A. E. Harting, vol 7. New Haven, 1986.

Redstone, B. V. 'The Carmelites of Ipswich.' *PSIA* 10 (1898-1900): 189-196.

Rosenthal, J. 'Kings, Continuity and Ecclesiastical Benefaction in the Fifteenth Century.' In *People, Politics, and Continuity in the Later Middle Ages*, edited by J. Rosenthal and C. Richmond, 166-177. Stroud, 1987.

Ruether, R. 'Misogynism and Virginal Feminism in the Fathers of the Church.' In *Religion and Sexism: Images of Woman in the Jewish and Christian Traditions*, edited by R. Ruether, 150-183. New York, 1974.

Rumble, A. *Domesday Book Suffolk*. A Survey of the Counties of England Volume 34. General ed. J. Morris. Chichester: 1986.

Russell, J. C. 'The Clerical Population of Medieval England.' *Traditio* 2 (1944): 177-212.

Rye, W. *Carrow Abbey, otherwise Carrow Priory; near Norwich, in the County of Norfolk*. Norwich, 1889.

Rye, W., ed. *The Visitation of Norfolk, Made and Taken by William Hervey, Clarenceaux King of Arms, Anno 1563*. London, 1891.

Rye, W. *A Short Calendar of the Deeds Relating to Norwich enrolled in the Court Rolls of that City, 1285-1306*. Norwich, 1903.

Rye, W. and E. A. Tillet. 'An Account and Description of Carrow Abbey, Norwich, together with an Appendix of Charters.' *Norwich: Norfolk Miscellany* 2 (1883): 465-508.

Savine, A. *English Monasteries on the Eve of the Reformation*. Oxford, 1909.

Salzman, L. F., ed. *The Victoria History of the County of Cambridge and the Isle of Ely*, vol. 2. London, 1948.

Scarfe, N. *Suffolk Landscape*. London, 1972.

Shahar, S. *The Fourth Estate: A History of Women in the Middle Ages*. London, 1983.

Sherlock, D. 'Excavations at Campsea Ash Priory.' *PSIA* 32:2 (1971): 121-139.

Smallwood, J. 'A Medieval Tile Kiln at the Abbey Farm, Shouldham.' *East Anglian Archaeology* 8 (1978): 45-54.

Smith, T., Smith, L. T., and Bretano, L. eds. *English Gilds*. Early English Text Society 40, 1890.

Snape, R. H. *English Monastic Finances in the Later Middle Ages*. New York: Barnes and Noble, 1926.

Southern, R. W. *Western Society and the Church in the Middle Ages*. London, 1970.

Tanner, N. *The Church in Late Medieval Norwich*. Toronto, 1984.

Taylor, R.C., ed. *Index Monasticus: or the Abbeys and Other Monasteries, Alien Priories, Friars, etc., in the Diocese of Norwich*. London, 1821.

Thompson, A. H., ed. *Visitations of Religious Houses in the Diocese of Lincoln*, 3 vols. London, 1915-1927.

Thompson, S. *Women Religious: The Founding of English Nunneries after the Norman Conquest*. Oxford, 1991.

Tillotson, J. *Marrick Priory: A Nunnery in Late Medieval Yorkshire*. York: Borthwick Papers, no. 75, 1989.

Tymms, S. ed. *Wills and Inventories from the Registers of the Commisary of Bury St Edmunds and the Archdeaconry*. London, 1850.

Warren, A. *Anchorites and their Patrons in Medieval England*. California, 1985.

Zimmerman, B. 'The White Friars at Ipswich.' *PSIA* 10 (1891-1900): 196-20.

Index

abbesses/ prioresses, lodgings, 38; privileges, 27-28; wills, 49; see *seigneurial*
accounts, of nunneries, 66
administration, by women, 17; in nunneries, 55-57
Aelfwen, 74
Alman, Margaret, 65
almsgiving, 63-64; see *charity; wills*
anchoresses, lifestyle, 18, Table 4, 74-78
anchorholds, 75; archaeology of, 76-77
Appleyard, Bartholomew of, 14, 61
archaeology, of nunneries, survival, 31; sources, 31; see *buildings, precincts, Gazetteer*; of informal communities, 73; of anchoresses, 76-77
Arundel, Isabel of, 24, 25
Ashfield, Robert, 61
Aslack, William, 62

Bale, John, 73
Barbara, Saint, 26, 27, 82
Bardolf, Sir John, 60
Baxster, Margery, 78
Beauchamp, Katherine, 47; Margaret, Guy, 51
Beccles, Suffolk, 69
beguinages, 19-20, 72; see *informal communities*
Berry, Edmund, Knight, 65
Blackborough, Norfolk, 23, 26; buildings, 33, 36; description, 83; patronage, 60

Blessed Virgin Mary, dedications, 26; icongraphy, 42; seals, 28-30, 90-91
Blickling, Robert, 62
books, in nunneries, 53-54
Boteler, Lady Katherine, 65
Boys, Sir Roger de, 60
Brandon, Suffolk, 22
Bruisyard, Suffolk, 23, 31, 33, 34; description, 89; patronage 57, 59, 60
buildings, at nunneries, construction, 31, 42, 86, 91; outer courts, 33; kitchens, 36, 83; east range, chapter-house, 84, 88; west range, guest house, 36, 45, 84-85, 86, 90; see *precincts; Gazetteer*
Bungay, Suffolk, 24; seal, 29, Plate 1; precinct wall, 31; church, 40; cloister, 42; description, 89-90; patronage 59-60
burial, at nunneries, 38, 62, 85, 89, 90
Bury St Edmunds, Suffolk, 22; hospitals, 69; anchorites, 75
Buttery, Ela, 49

Calle, Richard, 65
Calthorpe, Dorothy; Sir Philip, 48
Cambridge, St Radegund's, 24
Campsey Ash, Suffolk, 23, 33; mill, 34; church excavation, 40; fishponds, 34; west range, pentice, 42, Plate 10; description, 90-91; nuns, 50; library 54; patronage, 58-60; seal, 29; chantry, 59
Carbrooke, Norfolk, 69, 70

112

Carmelites, 74
Carrow, Norfolk, 23; latrine, 36; west range, 38, Figure 5, Plate 5; church, 40, 42, 57; description, 83-85; nuns, 48; seal, 28
Castleacre, Mary; John, 51
Catherine, Saint, 26, 27, 82
chantries, 59
charity, 70-71, 73; see *almsgiving*
Charles, Alice, 65
Cheselden, Alice de, 65
Chich, Essex, 21
churches, nunnery, 40, 42, 83-84, 86, 87, 88; laity at, 38, 40, 63; parish, 38, 89, 91
Clarence, Lionel Duke of, 24, 59
Clifton, Katherine; Sir Adam, 48
cloister, 42; orientation, 42; iconography, 42, 45
Cobb, Margery, 53-54
Cocket, Bridget, 55
commemoration, 49
Cook, Alice; John, 49
corrodians, 17, 65-66; accommodation, 38
Crabhouse, Norfolk, 23, 26; fishponds, 34; landscape, 25; survey of 1557, 31, 36, Figure 3; water source, 35; west range, 38; outbuildings, 33; cloister, 42; description, 85-86; origins, 77; anchoresses, 77; seal, 30
Creyk, Margery de, 24, 63

dedications, nunneries, 26-27; hospitals, 69-70
Denny, Cambridgeshire, 35, 73
Dereham, Baldwin, 79; Jane, Thomas, Isabel, 50
Domesday Book, nuns, 22, 79

Dunwich, Suffolk, 69

East Dereham, Norfolk, 21
Elstisley, Cambridgeshire, 21
Elstow, Bedfordshire, 34
Ely, Cambridgeshire, 21
Emma, of Redlingfield, 24
episcopal visitations, 56
Etheldreda, Saint, 21

fairs, 28
Fastolf, Cecil, 49
Felbrigge, Anne, 53
female piety, characteristics of, 13, 21, 81; landscapes of, 25; material culture of, 45; tradition of, 21-22
female saints, dedications to, 27, 82; of East Anglia, 21-22; iconography, 78; prayers to, 79
Fermer, Alice, 49
Fincham, Elizabeth, 54
fish, fishponds, at nunneries, 34-35
Fitzpiers, Geoffrey, 24
Flixton, Suffolk, 23, 33; corrodians, 36; seal, 29; description, 91
Folcard, Margaret; John, 48

Gernoun, Sir Nicholas, 60
Glanville, Gundreda de, 24
guests, at nunneries, 36, 45, 65
guilds, at nunneries, 61-62

Harsyk, Margery, 66-67
hermit, female, lifestyle, 18
Hermit, Isabella, 56
Heveningham, Suffolk, 78
Hingham, Norfolk, 79-80
historiography, of religious women, 20-22
Hord, Roger; Pamela, 65

113

hospitals, 68-71, 80
hospital sister, lifestyle, 14, 70, Table 2
Howard, Sir John, 62
Hunston, Thomas, 63

Ickleton, Cambridgeshire, 40
infirmary, 85, 88-89
informal communities, religious women, 17, Table 3, Plate 11, 71 74; archaeology of, 73
inner courts, at nunneries, 36-38
Ipswich, informal communities, 17, 71, 73-74

Jerves, Katherine, 55
Julian, of Norwich, 13, 18, 75, 76-77

Kemp, Margery, 13, 21
Kerdeston, Lady Margaret, 65
Keroyle, Edmund, 60; Margaret, 63
kiln, Shouldham, 35
King, Anne, 50

landscapes, eremetic, 18, 25; of nunneries, 23, 25-6; urban, 23
latrines, at nunneries, 35, 83-84; see *water management*
Leva, of Lynn, 24, 25, 77
Lyng, Norfolk, 25, 87
Lyon, Agnes, 70

Mann, Katherine, 74, 75-76
Marchaunt, William, 66
Marham, Norfolk, 23; earthworks, 33, 34, Plate 2; sculpture, 38, Figure 4; west range, 38; church, 40; pentice cloister, 42, Plate 7; description, 86-87; patronage, 60
Mary Magdalen, 69

Mason, Barbara, 49
Massingham, Norfolk, 77
Maud, Countess of Ulster and Oxford, 47, 51, 59, 62
mills, at nunneries, 28, 34, 66
moats, at nunneries, 33
monasteries for women, see *nunneries*
moniales, 79
'mother', 19, Table 6, 80
mystics, female, 13; literature, 54

north, female associations, 42, 45, 77, 82
Norwich, religious women, Black friars, 74, 75; Conisford, 75, 76; Elmhill, 73-74; St Giles (Great Hospital), 67, 70; St Paul's Hospital, 70; St Peter Hungate, 71, 72, 73; St Lawrence, 71; St Saviour, 76; St Stephen, 73; St Swithen, 17; Westwyk, 72
novices, 52
nuns, lifestyle, 14, 51-56; numbers, 46; prosopography, 47; social status, 47-50; geographical origins, 50; ages, 51; ex-nuns, 73
nunneries (monasteries for women), Table 1; filiation, 14; dates, 23; setting, 23; founders, 24; endowments, 24; dedications, 26; archaeology, 31-41

obedientiaries, 54-56
offices, Divine, 52
Oldham, Margaret, 77
Osyth, Saint, 21

Pandon, Saint, 22
Paston, Margery, 65
patronage, 57

Peakirk, Cambridgeshire, 22
Pega, 22, 25
Pellet, John, 17, 73
pentice cloister, 42
piety, of nuns, 58; of anchoresses, 78; of vowesses, 79; see *female piety*
Plaiz, Sir John, 60
precincts, of nunneries, boundaries, 31; outer courts, inner courts, 33; production, 34-5

Redlingfield, Suffolk, 23, 33; buildings, 33, 36, Plates 3-4; church, 40, 42; description, 91-92; seal, 28
Rich, John, 72

saints, see *female saints, dedications, seals*
Sampson, Grace, 49
Saxon, religious women, 21-22; archaeology, 22
Saxthorpe, Norfolk, 76
Scales, Muriel de, 24; Roger, Lord of, 60
sculpture, Marham, 38, Figure 4
seals, of nunneries, 28-30, Plate 1
Seething, Norfolk, 22
seigneurial rights, of nunneries, 27-28
self-sufficiency, of nunneries, 35
servants, in nunneries, 66
Shouldham, Norfolk, 23; precinct, 33, 34; kiln, 35; church, cropmarks 40-42, Plate 9; description, 87; patronage, 60
Simonds, Katherine, 48
Stanford, Albin of, 76
Stephen, King, 24
Stevenson, Elizabeth, 66
Studefield, Elizabeth; Sebastian, 48

Suffield, Bishop Walter of, 77
Suffolk, Isabel, Countess of, 57, 58, 62; Robert, Earl of, 58-59, 62
symbolism, see *cloisters, landscapes, sculpture, seals, female saints*

terminology, of religious women 19-20
Thetford, Norfolk, 23, 31, 34, 40, 42; foundation, 25; description, 87-89
Throckmorton, Elizabeth, 73
Trussbutt, Thomas, 61
Tunstead, Friar Simon, 62

Ufford, Maud de, 90; Edmund, 59, 62; chapel, 90

Valoine, Agnes, Joan de, 24
vocation, 14, 18-19, 20, 68-69, 79
vowesses, lifestyle, 18-19, Table 5, 78-79

water management, at nunneries, 35-36
Watton, Humbs, Gilbertine double house, 42
West Dereham, Norfolk, 79-80
widows, see *vowesses*
Wigginhall, Mary Magdalen, Norfolk, 77
Wigginhall, St Mary the Virgin, Norfolk, 78
wills, 10; religious women in, 19, 47-50, 60-61, 71, 79
Winfrith, 22
Wingfield, Robert, 50
Withburga, Saint, 21
women religious, categories of, 13; distribution of, Figures 1-2, 15-16, Tables 1-6; Church attitudes towards, 21, 78, 82

Wychingham, Sir William, 60
Wygun, Isabel, 84-85

Yaxle, Margaret, 54